Majolica Figures
Helen Cunningham

Schiffer Publishing Ltd

77 Lower Valley Road, Atglen, PA 19310

Dedication

This book is dedicated to my husband, Ben, and to our children Mera and Barrett, all of whom share my love for majolica. Without their patience and help, this book would never have made it to publication. Their love and moral support kept this project on target!

Copyright © 1997 by Helen Cunningham
Library of Congress Catalog Card Number: 96-71097

Printed in China

ISBN: 0-7643-0214-0

Book Design by Audrey L. Whiteside

Published by Schiffer Publishing Ltd.
77 Lower Valley Road
Atglen, PA 19310
(610) 593-1777
Fax (610) 593-2002
Please write for a free catalog.
This book may be purchased from the publisher.
Please include $2.95 for shipping.
Try your bookstore first.

We are interested in hearing from authors
with book ideas on related subjects.

Contents

Acknowledgments

This book began as a quest for information on my beloved Sarreguemines character jugs. When I had the opportunity to visit the Sarreguemines Museum for the first time several years ago, I had no idea what to expect. Upon my arrival I met with Mr. Emile Decker, conservateur of the Musée de Sarreguemines and his assistant, Mr. Christian Thevenin. I am deeply indebted to both of them as well as to their staff and to Mr. Denis Bour, president of Les Amis Du Musée Et Des Arts De Sarreguemines (Friends of the Museum and the Arts of Sarreguemines) for the hospitality and genuine kindness they all extended to me. Their willingness to share their valuable time and knowledge impressed me beyond words. I have enjoyed Sarreguemines majolica for over twenty years, and now I feel the same warmth for the people associated with preserving the heritage of this wonderful factory. Without their generosity, responsiveness, and willingness to share resources, this book might never have developed. My sincere thanks to all of them.

As my quest continued, I searched for information on other factories. I am indebted to Bertrand Cocq of France for his interest in this project and his willingness to share vital information on the factories in the north of France. His help was truly invaluable. I am also indebted to "Marty" of the United Kingdom for sharing his time and his collection with me. I greatly appreciate his help in photographing pieces of his collection.

Maryse and Gerard Bottero were extremely generous in sharing information on the Massiers and other French factories with me. Their charming antique shop in Nice, France, and their personal collection served as an invaluable source of photos. I also wish to thank Robert Lehr of Paris for his kindness in discussing the Massier firm with me. Sophie Lehr opens her antique shop in Biot, France, during the summer months. Rita and Ian Smythe of Britannia at Grays Antique Market in London were extremely kind in providing photos of very hard to find pieces. Britannia is a majolica lover's paradise.

Joan Jones, Curator of the Minton Museum, Royal Doulton PLC, responded immediately to my request for information on Minton. I wish to thank her for her enthusiasm and her willingness to take her valuable time to send me examples of some exquisite Minton pieces, as well as necessary information on the factory.

I also wish to thank Michael Strawser of Majolica Auctions by Michael G. Strawser, whose help was immediate and forthcoming. I greatly appreciate his assistance with photos and information. Mary-Anne Smith, Public Relations Specialist for William Doyle Galleries Auctioneers & Appraisers, also provided much needed photos and information. In addition, many thanks to Nicolaus Boston of London for his help with information on some rare English pieces.

Without the help of friends like Gail Dearing of Dearing Antiques and Heirloom Wicker on Miami Circle in Atlanta, I would not have been able to include photographs of some very important pieces. I wish to thank Pam Ferrazzutti of Pam Ferrazzutti Antiques at Harbourfront Antiques Market in Toronto for her cooperation in obtaining photographs, and Dawna Layman of Leprechaun Antiques who kindly allowed me to take photographs of some wonderful examples of majolica in her booth at Don Scott's Antique Market in Atlanta. I also would like to acknowledge the cooperation of Jerry S. Hayes of Oklahoma City, Oklahoma, in photographing some noteworthy pieces. Other friends who shared information include Carolyn and Max Nickerson of Nickerson's Antiques. I am especially indebted to Everett Grist for his constant encouragement and wise advice regarding this book.

Special thanks to Joan B. Stacke for her encouragement and her help. I wish to thank collectors Cay and C. D. Gann, III, Brandon and Jeff Queen, and Gerri and Jim Trout of the United States; Jacques Salzard, Roger Barbat, Henriette and Philippe Bailet, along with other collectors in France who wish to remain anonymous; and Vic Schuler of London for their cooperation and assistance. I gratefully acknowledge the cooperation of Michael Ribero of the Musée de la Poterie, Vallauris, France, for allowing me to take photographs in his museum and Ester Schneider, General Director of the Villeroy & Boch Archives in Mettlach, Germany, for her help in researching a letter that I felt was necessary to include in this book. Thanks, too, go to Virginia Khouri, the librarian at Cheekwood-Tennessee Botanical Gardens and Museum of Art for her help in research.

The keen and discerning eye of interior decorator Anne Ford of Anne Ford Associates, Inc., in Nashville led her to purchase some fabulous pieces of majolica for her clients, and I was fortunate that she allowed me to photograph them. I also wish to thank Amy Frierson, Director of the Houston Museum of Decorative Arts in Chattanooga, Tennessee, for her cooperation. My sincere gratitude to Jill Graham of New York City for her wonderful contribution of illustrations to this book. Arnold Kowalsky was kind enough to share resources with me, and I wish to extend my thanks.

The assistance of Sam Jordan of Dury's Professional Photographic Supplies and the staff at Chromatics PhotoImaging Services in Tennessee helped immensely. My sisters-in-law Patricia Devoto, Joanne Walker, and Elaine Cartland offered their editorial and artistic expertise and I am indebted to them. I am also indebted to my brother, Joe Cartland, for his unfailing enthusiasm. Constant moral support came from Brenda and Don Wilson. I wish to thank Lieselotte W. Regen for her assistance with the graphics.

Last but most importantly, I wish to express my sincere gratitude to Nancy and Peter Schiffer of Schiffer Publishing, Ltd., for their interest in this project. They helped me fine-tune my ideas and were always cheerful and patient with my questions. I also would like to thank Jeffrey Snyder for his assistance in polishing this manuscript.

Preface

The Quest: A Collector's Passion

This book began as a quest for information on Sarreguemines character jugs and other majolica figures. As a collector, the quest for additions to my collection rivaled the desperate need for facts concerning the factories themselves. While a number of wonderful books on majolica exists, none covers majolica figures or toby jugs in any great detail.

Although I could find some information on the English factories, I could find only a limited amount or none at all on many of the French factories. As a collector I was curious to know just how I might direct my collection, but I could not find enough information to detail my options. I had numerous questions regarding the scope of figural productions by the various majolica manufacturers.

Why were certain figures duplicated by manufacturers in different countries, while others were produced exclusively at a particular factory? Why do French jugs often have red or turquoise interiors? Were most of the figures stereotypical of the period or were they of particular individuals? Were they commissioned or merely produced in the hopes that they would appeal to the consumer?

Even the terminology seemed difficult to understand. Some people referred to any piece that had a figure as "figural," while others used the term solely to indicate a jug entirely in the shape of an animal. Some collectors use the word "majolica" and "faïence" interchangeably. Other confusing terms included "copy" and "reproduction."

In addition to these concerns, I was curious about majolica in the cultural context. What factors influenced the manufacturers? What about the nineteenth century made the consuming public so receptive to the introduction of majolica in general, and of figures in particular?

This book is intended to answer many of these questions. In an effort to explain the immediate success of majolica and to understand the likes and dislikes of the consuming public of the nineteenth century, it is necessary to study the artistic trends and the interrelationship of the arts at the time. An overview of history, art, literature, and the stylistic changes taking place during the century will aid in a better understanding of the acceptance of majolica and of specific figures.

The nineteenth century witnessed an unprecedented interdependency within the arts and a novel relationship between the artist and the public. Majolica appeared on the scene to a middle class public already prepared to accept the unusual. However, its acceptance goes much deeper than that. By examining the fine arts as well as the decorative arts, one can better understand the cultural environment and the role played by majolica.

When considering majolica figures, it is impossible to include all figures. Instead, I have selected figures that are indicative of the artistic and cultural framework of the century. I have also tried to show at least some examples from each factory that offered much variety in figures. In so doing I hope to give the reader a greater appreciation of the century historically and thus a greater appreciation of the reasoning behind the manufacture of these figures.

In addition I hope to give the reader some expertise in deciding if a figure is authentic or if it is a reproduction. The popularity of certain designs continues today. These reproductions, however honestly marked, are sometimes mistakenly sold as originals, because the average collector of figures and even some dealers are unaware of the telltale indicators of the original productions. A general understanding of the palettes, thickness of potting, detail in modeling, and frequency of design by these manufacturers will perhaps help prevent unintentional errors.

Although England produced large quantities of majolica in the second half of the nineteenth century, only a very few of the factories offered much variety in the way of figures. English productions of pottery figures consisted mostly of earthenware like the Staffordshire "peasant art," or of creamware, pearlware, and stoneware like the old toby jugs. Minton, the creator of the English majolica, and his follower George Jones were the primary English manufacturers to offer much variety in the way of majolica figures.

France, on the other hand, produced an extensive array of figures, the majority of which were made of majolica. The variety and ingenuity of these French producers make for very interesting study. Sarreguemines was by far the largest pottery manufacturer in France and carried a very wide range of quality products, including majolica figures. Prices on these figures continue to rise as more and more collectors discover the fine quality and technical expertise invested in these wares.

On the continent some manufacturers produced and marked their majolica figures, but these were made in limited quantities in most cases. Other continental manufacturers, however, had large lines of majolica figures but did not mark their wares. Cottage industries account for a large part of the unmarked majolica manufacturing on the continent at the turn of the twentieth century.

Both England and countries on the continent produced figures in porcelain, but I will deal with porcelain and earthenware figures only in that they influenced the designs for majolica figures. Some of the older designs were continued in majolica, but many of the majolica figural designs were original.

Herein a liberal definition of majolica is used. Because collectors of majolica figures usually have a wide variety within their collections, it is important to include not only traditional majolica (which is a soft, porous clay, fired to a biscuit stage, and covered with a tin or lead glaze before refiring), but also parian and earthenware figures with a majolica glaze and even some faïence. Faïence, technically understood to be the predecessor to majolica, consists of a finer clay with a stanniferous (tin-oxide) glaze followed by a clear glaze. Though rarely included in books on majolica, faïence is the French word used to mean majolica and therefore must be included in a study of French figures.

For the sake of this book, I will use the word "figure" to mean any piece that has a three-dimensional, high relief figure of a human (real or imagined) or animal occupying at least 60% of the piece. Auction catalogs generally list as figurals any piece consisting of 75% or more in the shape of a figure, but the term is subjective. In instances where the figure is the primary feature of the design but does not quite meet the 60% stipulation, it is included because of the importance of the figure relative to the piece itself. Figural strikers, for example, are commonly referred to by the name of the figure upon them. These figures usually represent only about 50% of the piece but are important to any study of figures.

The term "toby" generally means any pitcher in the shape of a person, though technically it describes only a jug in the shape of an entire human or fictional figure. "Character" jug identifies a piece in the shape of a head or head and shoulders only.

This book is not intended as a complete guide for majolica figures or as a technical history of pottery manufacturing. Instead it is intended as a cultural and social guide to the period of majolica figural production in the hopes that others will share my love and genuine appreciation of these charming pieces, each with a personality of its own!

Pricing Information

The price guide is intended only as general reference. Though the range included is derived from actual selling prices, both from auctions and from shops, prices are always affected by condition, coloring, detail, size, rarity, and above all collectibility. For example, solid colored jugs or figures are often more rare, but they never bring as much as the polychromed ones. They are simply not as collectible. Very often the rarest pieces sell below value because they are not common enough to be recognized, so collectors will pass on them in favor of the more recognizable examples. Often these more common ones bring far beyond their value for the same reason: They are familiar.

I have strived for an average price range of examples in very good condition. Exceptionally mint pieces will realize higher prices. While chips or minor damage should not deter the collector from buying a piece, they should be clearly reflected in the price. Whenever possible, it is best to buy pieces in as near perfect condition as the budget allows. However, some figures are so rare that damage is overlooked. Some photos herein are given to make a point and no price is available; these have NP in the caption, meaning "no price."

Majolica prices are variable. Overall they are rising steadily, especially on the better pieces. At any given time, however, it is difficult to put a simple price on a piece of majolica. I feel that a price range will hopefully give consumers a better idea of relative values. Remember that the prices quoted in the price guide are retail prices. If selling or buying wholesale, the price should be about half of the quoted prices. Dealers spend a great deal of time and effort obtaining pieces and have a great deal of overhead.

They must receive compensation for their time, effort, and knowledge. Never begrudge a dealer his or her profit. They have earned it! Moreover, do not expect a dealer to pay the price quoted in this guide. These prices represent their selling prices.

Prices, of course, vary according to the section of the country, and even the country itself. Prices for French pieces are generally higher in France than for the same piece in the United States. On the other hand, English pieces often bring more in the United States than in England. Much depends upon the concentration of collectors. Within the United States, it follows that in the Northeast where greater demand exists, prices rise accordingly. In fact, prices are sometimes twice as high as what one might expect to pay for the same piece in the Midwest or the South.

It is impossible to put a price on museum pieces or on extremely rare examples of figures, so no prices are given for these pieces. Some figures, while not particularly rare, are very hard to find because they are cross-collected. For example, collectors of railroad items may want to buy the Onnaing railroad jug even though they do not collect jugs or majolica. Likewise, collectors of Napoleonic pieces sometimes drive up the prices on pieces in this category. Collectors of these items sometimes push prices beyond what majolica collectors think reasonable.

Female figures generally cost slightly more than their male counterparts because fewer models were made. The small Sarreguemines toby jugs often cost as much the larger ones because not as many have survived.

Prices quoted are in U. S. Dollars.

Introduction

Setting the Stage: An Overview of the Nineteenth and Early Twentieth Centuries

During the first third of the nineteenth century England was in the enviable position of having already begun industrialization. Ideally situated as a port and with abundant natural resources, the Industrial Revolution as well as colonization moved England forward at a rapid pace economically. She became a world leader, a position maintained as Queen Victoria came to the throne in 1837. Victoria reigned in an atmosphere of prosperity and stability.

The middle of the century was well underway before it witnessed the beginning of the Industrial Revolution in France. The French Revolution and the subsequent "Reign of Terror" had delayed industrialization there. The Napoleonic Wars that followed and short reigns by two kings slowed economic development.

In 1830 Louis-Phillipe, who had lived in America, brought his republican ideas with him to the throne of France. The Chamber of Deputies declared him "King of the French by Grace of God and the will of the people."[1] However, the revolution of workers in Paris in 1848 created a class war in which 10,000 workers were killed, leading to the establishment of the Second Republic and representation in government for the working class. The revolution had caused many French laborers to emigrate to England where they were warmly received because of the English interest in decorative arts.[2]

The United States, meanwhile, had just elected Martin Van Buren, the first president born in the new "United States of America" rather than Colonial America. At this time the emerging nation was struggling with growing pains as it expanded its frontiers westward. This expansion, followed by the Civil War, delayed the development of industrialization in America until the last third of the century.

By the end of the nineteenth century and the first part of the twentieth century other European countries, especially Germany, were becoming major economic competitors for England. As not only Germany, but also the United States, Japan, Belgium, Italy, and the Netherlands became increasingly industrialized, Britain began having to share her position as world leader. The colonization and years of contentment that had taken place during the nineteenth century came to a close with World War I.

The Social Scene

With each country's industrialization came more urbanization. The old footpaths or walking streets of the eighteenth-century cities became stagecoach routes during the first third of the nineteenth century. In England the invention of steam powered locomotives in 1830 rapidly increased the migration of workers from rural areas to urban areas where they found greater opportunities. The demand for labor and the expanding factories enabled more and more people to live in relative comfort.

Industrialized countries increasingly became countries of more than just two classes. A healthy economy contributed to a reduction in class tension and to pride in industry. The rising middle class became involved in politics and the "bourgeois capitalist" became someone of status.

The purchasing power of this new middle class began to change the social scene. Factory owners and brewers had titles bestowed on them. Becoming an earl or a duke placed them on the same social level as military heroes, lawyers, and lord chancellors.[3]

The increase in wages of skilled and unskilled workers created a segment of society that lived in relative comfort with some disposable income and some leisure to enjoy it. Parks developed, concerts abounded, and libraries opened. The gap between the classes began to narrow.

Larger sections of the middle class began ruling the arts and politics, thus changing the face of society. This new found status created consumers who desperately sought luxury in order to display their new found wealth. Though they still could not afford the finery of the aristocracy, they could buy better quality products than ever before. This new middle class sought bigger and better houses with larger and more luxurious furniture, lighting, and decorations.

The light clothing and heavy furniture of the first part of the century reversed. The furniture became lighter and more intricately carved, while the clothes became heavier. The days of gauzy, high-waisted dresses were waning as better textile manufacturing created more elaborate fabrics. The waist lowered, the fabrics became thicker, the skirts multiplied, and their circumference increased. Brocades and velvets "announced" one's wealth. The freedom of spirit of the Empire period gave way to the need for fancy in the Victorian era. Hats, feathers and jewelry appeared to "decorate" the middle class.

Perhaps one reason that clothes became heavier was for warmth. Unlike the luxurious homes of the aristocracy, the middle class coal-heated houses were dark and drafty from ill-fitting doors and windows. Women began wearing as many as six layers of skirts. Velvets were not only luxurious, but warmer. Even at the theater warmer clothes were necessary as gas heat required ventilation. Leaving the doors open during the performance meant that the ladies needed muffs inside as well as outside.[4]

Colors became as important as the choice of fabric. Since gas lighting cast a dim, yellowish hue, perhaps warmer colors appealed to the Victorians. It is easy to see why the brightly colored majolica was such a commercial success, since it contrasted with the somber surroundings.

In the 1830s F. W. Woolworth went to Europe to buy seconds of china which ordinarily were destroyed. He brought them to the United States originally to sell to the landed gentry, but as the middle class "carriage trade" began buying them, he opened his "5 & 10" stores. By the 1840s, china emporiums, like Woolworth's, began opening in all towns.[5]

Guidelines developed for using particular pieces of china for each dinner course, thus requiring that the Victorian household have an enormous variety of tableware. By the 1880s decorating magazines included majolica, suggesting which courses required majolica rather than china.

Education of the "Mass Public"

In 1855 when the news stamp tax was abolished in England, inexpensive newspapers were distributed rapidly through railways. The steam press, telegraph, and cable made dissemination of news quicker as well. Because of newspapers and a better informed public, novelty became a way of life. The public liked change just for its own sake, perhaps accounting for the success of majolica. It contrasted sharply with the pottery and porcelain of the day.

With newspapers, libraries, and access to better schools, the middle class stayed informed. Educational opportunities now existed for the middle class, not just the upper class. Manners and consumption grew closer. An elite society no longer existed, but rather a "mass public." Steady streams of visitors to museums and galleries necessitated mixing the aristocracy with the bourgeois and foreigners.

In 1841 the London Library opened and by 1870 a large clientele enjoyed 80,000 volumes in circulation. Only 20% of the population was now illiterate compared with 75% in 1812. In 1870 the Education Act established a tax-funded educational system throughout England.[6] Oxford and Cambridge broadened their curriculums and allowed entrance to upper middle class students.

This new society, however, lacked the standards required to judge art and elegance and was uncertain with regard to taste. Trends, consequently, changed quickly as consumers feared being considered unfashionable.

The need for acceptance created a consuming public that latched onto each new fashion trend with such alacrity that the manufacturers constantly felt the need to create something exciting and different. A frenzied desire to display created enthusiasm for the eclectic. Consumers tried to be first to "discover" a new fashion.

Multitudes of factory-made knickknacks began filling the Victorian homes. Furniture groupings and sets of pottery representing "the Fates" or "the Seasons" became stylish. Collecting escalated as the middle class families wanted to leave their mark on society and desired objects for their legacies.

This mass public wanted class as well as money, and manners became essential. Specific sets of standards ruled a rigid society. The wealthiest people were the great landowners, but a middle class of clerks, retailers, factory foremen, and professors stressed industry and thrift. Perhaps these industrious masses turned to religion for a set of rules, because the rigid moral code of the Victorians resembled rules taught by nuns in Catholic schools.

This rigid code controlled every aspect of society. An article in a *Punch* magazine from the 1850s commented that while a lady could perform a quadrille with "a member of the country," she should only waltz with a peer.[7] The moral code was even more rigid in the lower classes who tried to stress their respectability. The religious movement believed in two classes: the godly and the ungodly. Faith and temperance movements evolved.

The Victorian passion for respectability had allowed little latitude for conduct. It was not until the 1890s that the moral taboos began to disappear following a decline in religious beliefs and less emphasis on church attendance. The change in attitude toward church attendance arose as museums and art galleries started opening on Sunday afternoons.

Museums and galleries created new sources of inspiration for pottery designers. Often new figurals appeared using designs or color in a manner not unlike a recent exhibit. A knowledge of the period often helps one date majolica figures by subject matter or by coloring.

The End of Optimism

The prosperity of the mid century climaxed as the century approached its last third. Britain maintained leadership in world trade with a value greater than the trade of France, Germany, and Italy combined. The world, nonetheless, was changing at a rapid pace. The depressions during the last third of the nineteenth century ended the optimism of the Victorians. With increased trade competition from Germany and the United States, the British realized they were not the only industrialized nation. The English economy continued to rise, but it was not with the same rapidity that consumers had experienced in the first two-thirds of the century.

Although labor unions had organized around the middle of the century, it was not until the last third that mechanization became a real threat, strengthening the need for unions. Despite the depressions and strikes, however, people still lived in relative comfort and contentment. Life had become easier because of the advancements in technology.

Britain sold quantities of textiles, coal, and ships to Europe, America, and the East. This same trade, however, created less of a dependency on Britain. With their own ships, other countries were less dependent on trade with Britain, yet Britain refused to protect her trade by tariffs. This free trade policy allowed for import of cheaper goods from overseas, and left British agriculture unprotected. The development of railroads, steamships, and refrigeration meant goods could be imported from greater and greater distances. Other countries protected their industries by tariffs imposed on British goods.

Even though Britain was a leader in industry and agriculture, she could not compete with America. The invention of farming machinery for prairie farming and the improved ocean transportation allowed cheap American wheat to flood the British market.[8] As British agriculture collapsed, rural laborers migrated to towns. With this tremendous influx of people and the ensuing depressions came poverty and slums in the cities.

Although many social problems existed in England and on the continent during the nineteenth century, they did not overshadow the sense of pride in the accomplishments of the period. This pride caused a confidence in life itself which helped relieve class tensions. The revolution of this century was the Industrial Revolution. An atmosphere of prosperity and stability strengthened the belief in the work ethic. Self-improvement and self-discipline set the standards of the time.

Entertainment in the Nineteenth and Early Twentieth Centuries

The middle class, now a "mass public" with increased leisure time, expected entertainment. There were "Punch and Judy" puppet shows, special art exhibits, and natural history exhibits at local museums. Libraries expanded their collections as more and more people could read. Newspapers grew in circulation, though they still appealed to the masses with sensationalism. At first the bourgeoisie copied the aristocracy, but eventually they developed tastes of their own.

The subject matter of majolica figurals reflected the new awareness of the middle class. Punch and Judy figures became popular pieces in earthenware and in majolica. Politicians appeared in pottery if newspapers carried stories about them. Toby jugs included not only politicians, but also popular representational figures like John Bull.

As lighting improved, theaters could dim the house lights and the audience paid more attention to the performance rather than constantly looking for the latest in fashion. The advent of electricity provided better heating and greater comfort at the theater; consequently, attendance increased. Actors and playwrights became trendy topics of conversation.

The bourgeoisie liked concerts and theater, which emerged as the most popular forms of entertainment of the period. At the end of the century 7.5 million Parisians attended the theater once a week and one million attended once a month. In fact, the prize for the Paris-Brest bicycle race in 1891 was a reserved place at the Opera. Popular actors and comedians materialized in majolica. Dranem, a turn of the century comedian, was immortalized in pottery by both Sarreguemines and Nimy.

By the end of the century, cafe-concerts serving beverages along with entertainment became popular in France. They attracted a wide variety of attendees, including women and children. A different version of the English public house, the cafe-concerts became the competitor of the theater.

The glamour of travel appealed to the middle class. Jules Verne's *Around the World in 80 Days* inspired an audience of followers. The first *Michelin* Guide for travelers was printed in 1900. Beaches like the French Riviera and ski resorts became popular retreats for the upper and middle classes.[9] This newfound awareness of exotic places created interest in pottery figures in ethnic costumes, as well as interest in exotic animals.

As the century drew to a close, the tight reign on morality began to loosen, attitudes became freer, and more diversity developed. In England majolica by this time had become overproduced and its popularity began to decline. However, such was not the case on the continent. World War I created new inspirations for the figural designers and figures from the war emerged in majolica, particularly in France.

This Sarreguemines griffin figural pitcher exemplifies the Napoleonic style with its lion's paw feet on a plinth base. $450-550

Chapter One

Stylistic Trends and the Pottery of the Period

The Empire and the Neo-Classical Periods

Pottery in the nineteenth century reflected the contemporary fashions in furniture and the decorative arts. The popular neo-classical designs in ornamentation complemented the Napoleonic style present at the end of the eighteenth century, since purity of line characterized both. The lion's paw feet on plinth bases and the low relief scroll of the Napoleonic designs will reappear later in the nineteenth century on some French majolica figures.

The potters at Wedgwood had achieved fame early in the eighteenth century for their neo-classical designs. French Sarreguemines wares of the period also carried similar designs. White or black relief designs reminiscent of ancient Greek and Roman themes contrasted with the plain, solid colored backgrounds.

As the century progressed, however, two diverse markets developed: the trendy sophisticated and the traditional popular markets. The sophisticated markets preferred porcelains like Meissen and Sèvres. The Meissen factory in Germany had rediscovered the Chinese art of manufacturing porcelain in the early eighteenth century. Meissen porcelains of rococo design along with the gracefully styled French Sèvres porcelains remained popular with the upper class at the turn of the century and served as inspiration for many future designs of majolica figures.

Rural designs included birds, landscapes, shells, and feathers found on popular wares including luster, mocha, and stoneware. Even Staffordshire blue and white transfer print wares sported such patterns. Chinese patterns dominated the Staffordshire wares until the early nineteenth century. Gradually designers turned to English subjects. Cities, lakes, and later Gothic ruins appeared. The transfer printing consisted of underglaze cobalt blue because it could withstand the high temperatures of the kiln. It was not until the late 1840s that the technology progressed enough to allow multi-colored underglaze printing.

The Gothic Revival

With the dawning of the nineteenth century had come a longing for the dreams and fairy tales of medieval times. Thus began the Gothic Revival in contrast to the eighteenth-century Neo-Classicism. The dreams of knights in shining armor coming to rescue a generation exhausted from turmoil seemed to appeal to the general public. Art and literature reflected this trend, as did the decorative arts.

The neo-classical designs so well known on Wedgwood jasperware felt competition from Gothic inspired relief-molded wares. Gothic motifs had originated in Italy in the mid-fifteenth century. The Hispano-Moresque pottery at this time carried an indecipherable faux Arabic script rather than actual lettering. These wares depicted heraldic animals, oak or acanthus leaves, and black lettered inscriptions.[1] Majolica manufacturers later used these gothically inspired designs.

The Baroque and Rococo Influence

Though the Baroque ideals originated in Italy and began as a reaction to classical rules, the term later became synonymous with the luxury and wealth depicted by the French King Louis XV. Baroque connotes lavish splendor like that exhibited in Versailles with its Hall of Mirrors, fabulous gardens, and fine porcelains. The Victorians sought to duplicate this finery in their own way. They loved elaborately designed decorations, highly carved furniture with curved lines, and fine clothes of rich fabrics.

Thus began what some call the "Second Baroque." This period, begun by Louis-Phillipe in France, spread to

England in 1845 when designers, decorators, and artists published pamphlets on design. About the same time "French Antique" became high style in the United States. French wallpaper and draperies filled American homes. The appeal of the Second Baroque spread quickly because of mass production.

The Second Baroque, or French Antique, became one of the most widely accepted styles in history. Everyday items like trivets, bottles, and packaging came under the spell of the style.[2] Potters used the curved lines and elegance of the Baroque style in their manufacturing of majolica figures.

The heavily gilded ceramics and the neo-classical motifs of the Empire period moved aside as Baroque and Rococo styles appeared. The cycles of styles repeat themselves. Baroque, and its descendent rococo, originated in the eighteenth century as a reaction to classical designs. Neoclassical followed rococo toward the end of the century and then the Second Baroque style developed. Yet each revival added a freshness and change of perspective that defined it.

Pottery manufacturers both in Britain and on the continent reveled in the wonderful designs offered by the Baroque and Rococo periods. Designs such as nymphs, shells, small birds, flowers, leaves, asymmetry, and curved scroll-work served as inspiration, but the nineteenth-century decorative arts added a playfulness lacking in the original. The Victorian interest in botany led to far more accuracy in design of the flowers added to lids or grouped on the bodies than those on earlier pieces.

The heavy, dramatic Empire furniture gave way to the reintroduction of painted furnishings like those of the Louis XV style. The "Second Baroque" style, fashioned after the elegant double curves of the Louis XV Baroque, remains perhaps the best known of the Victorian era. Louis XV furniture boasted beautiful cabriole legs and delicate curving backs.

It was not until the last third of the century that the classically influenced, somewhat simpler lines, reeded legs, and smoother curves of the Louis XVI style became high style. Decorative arts, of course, followed the styles of the day.

Buildings became more ornate and each Victorian home displayed as much as possible in order for the family to appear wealthy and important. "The more, the better" seemed to capture the spirit of the time. The first Baroque period demanded luxuries as proof of position. Perhaps the same applies to the Second Baroque. Pottery manufacturers took advantage of this attitude and constantly strived to create figures that would appeal to the consuming public.

The Naturalism of Mid Century

In a review of the Paris Exhibition of 1844 the term "running patterns" appeared. Suddenly by mid century the pottery often contained running plants or vines, not the bunched ones of Rococo. Genre scenes with human figures from everyday life began to appear on jugs. Sporting and drinking scenes, stag hunts, antler handles, and game appeared in the decorative arts.

Plants growing up the sides of pitchers and tree trunk handles typify mid century pottery. Other decorative arts incorporated the running patterns. Silver trays and flatware had twisted vines with birds or flowers. Even very classical decorative arts often had random patterns of vines. Majolica designs, of course, included similar motifs. On pitchers the weight moved toward the base, the lips began to curve, and a footring developed.[3]

Running plant patterns appeared on much of the decorative arts around the middle of the nineteenth century. This silver basket depicts the use of birds with the running plant pattern. NP

Naturalism's gentle, rococo-inspired curves contrasted with the formal, rather severe lines of the Gothic design. In this climate it is easy to see why Minton's majolica with its naturalistic patterns was such a success. What a welcome contrast to the Staffordshire and Rockingham wares popular with the middle class.

Monkeys have been used as figural designs in pottery since the 8th century B.C., but interest in them revived after the publication of Charles Darwin's *On The Origin of Species by Means of Natural Selection* in 1859. This pitcher combines the running pattern with the monkey design. Unattributed. *Courtesy of Bertrand Cocq* $300-500

A continental candleholder with a clinging monkey indicates the far-reaching popularity of monkeys as decoration. *Courtesy of Majolica Auctions by Michael G. Strawser* $450-650 pair

The naturalism of mid century combined with ancient patterns after the publication of Charles Darwin's *On the Origin of Species by Means of Natural Selection* in 1859. Staff finials of earthenware monkeys had been discovered in Egypt as early as 750 B.C., but a resurgence of interest in them occurred. Darwin was the grandson of Josiah Wedgwood, so perhaps it was inevitable that potters include primates in designs.

"Rebirth" of the Renaissance

As museums included Renaissance exhibits, with the *amorini* or infant cupids of High Italian Renaissance art and the cherubs of the French Renaissance, more and more pottery included similar figures, called *putti* (singular *putto*).

Putto is Italian for small boy. The term came to be applied to any childlike figure, male or female, human or pagan. Found in the decorative arts since classical times, the figures are usually winged making it difficult to distinguish whether they are amorini or cherubs.[4]

Other Renaissance decorations adapted the *grotesques* or half-figures. The name derived from the fact that these pieces were discovered in grottoes or caves. *Grotesques* based on Eastern designs were called *arabesques*. Renaissance designs also included interwoven ribbons, shells, figures with wings as extremities, caricatural dolphins, masks, and the classical acanthus leaf. Observers only need to examine Raphael's *Galatea* with its amorini, shells, dolphins, and grotesques to find the inspiration for many of the designs on majolica.

The nineteenth-century English and French potters, with typical innovation, adapted these designs. *Putti* began appearing holding shells or baskets aloft as candleholders, or riding dolphins which served as condiment dishes. Round-headed dolphins with upturned snouts became vases.

A Sarreguemines dolphin vase in the Renaissance taste with its upturned snout exhibits a sense of humor typical of the nineteenth century. *Courtesy of "Marty"* $250-325

Though not considered a figural, this Minton urn by Thomas Kirby, circa 1857, clearly depicts the Renaissance Revival style with its *putti* both as a figural and a painted design. *Courtesy of William Doyle Galleries Auctioneers & Appraisers* NP

Dolphins like these on a George Jones shell condiment illustrate the Victorian sense of novelty. 9" high. *Courtesy of Majolica Auctions by Michael G. Strawser* $1,000-1,400

The Oriental Influence

Trade with the Far East had begun when Marco Polo returned to Italy in the thirteenth century with porcelains and spices wrapped in silk or designed paper. It was this paper that brought painting to Europe. Chinese porcelains were being produced as early as the eighth century, but it took the Europeans several more centuries to discover the secret ingredient for making porcelain: Kaolin.

Products from the Orient had reached European homes through the Middle East until sea routes began opening in the sixteenth century. Even Columbus was seeking a sea route to the Far East. East India Companies formed for trade with the Orient. Large quantities of Chinese blue and white porcelains were imported, especially by the Dutch. Potters in the city of Delft imitated these wares, and Delft became famous for its blue and white faïence.

The imitations of the oriental style became a conglomerate of American Indian, African, Eastern Indian, and Chinese examples called *Chinoiserie*. Perhaps a more accurate term would be *Des Indes* indicating the entire range of designs based on the tales of travelers without much concern for accuracy. Hybrids evolved: exotic birds, feather headdresses, turbans, human figures, and pagodas combined in strange ways.[5] The appeal to the consuming public was enormous, and pottery as well as porcelain manufacturers were quick to capitalize on the market.

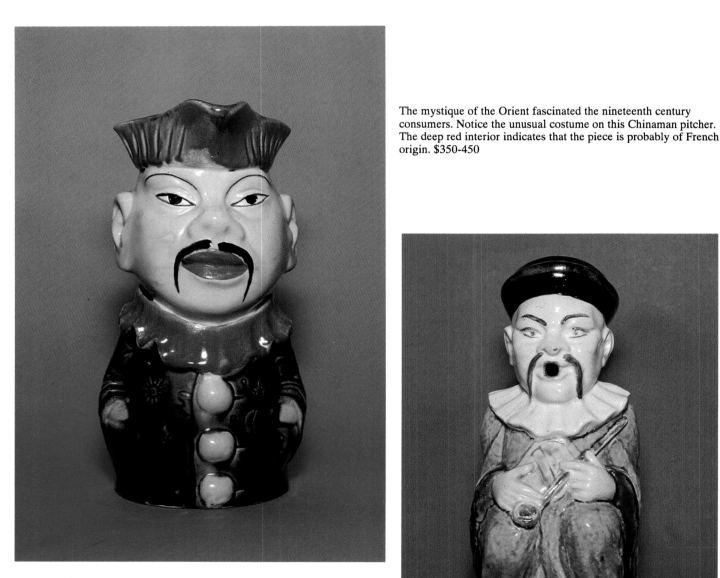

The mystique of the Orient fascinated the nineteenth century consumers. Notice the unusual costume on this Chinaman pitcher. The deep red interior indicates that the piece is probably of French origin. $350-450

This Chinaman pitcher appears somewhat more accurate in his dress. 10" high. *Courtesy of M. & G. Bottero Antiquites, Nice* $350-450

These Middle Eastern figures, one wearing a kaffiyeh and the other wearing a turban, exemplify the Des Indes designs. *Courtesy of Everett Grist* $125-200 each

Public interest in *Chinoiserie* designs waned as mid century approached. In 1846 a review by John Ridgway of a vase designed in the Chinese manner stated that it was "not of a class we desire to see multiplied."[6] By the late 1860s, however, the public seemed ripe for the revival of the Eastern styles.

When Commodore Matthew Perry, a United States naval commander, secured a formal trade agreement with Japan in 1854, Japanese products became available in both America and Europe. Since Japan had previously isolated itself, these new designs attracted a great deal of interest. The trend setting Chinese designs on the bone china of the early 1800s now reappeared as Japanese designs.

The South Kensington International Exhibition of 1862 and the Paris Exhibition of 1867 included Japanese wares. Japanese motifs with gold tracery began to appear on much of the decorative arts. A new restraint and formality had paralleled the exuberance of the naturalism in the 1860s, and this restraint adapted well to Japanese designs.

Though it retained its western shapes, pottery of the period had oriental decorations. Small sprays of flowers fashioned after Japanese decorating began to appear. Bamboo designs became borders or handles. The jugs of the mid century often had basketweave or wood designs for the surface, so oriental flowers complemented the texture and prunus blossoms appeared.

Majolica seemed a wonderful medium for use of Japanese-inspired artistry, which was enormously successful in the American market. The Philadelphia Centennial Exposition of 1876 created an export market for the majolica producers in Europe where Japanese motifs were readily consumed. By the 1880s there was a tremendous boom in the majolica market. The magnetism of Japanese prints continued to be felt in Europe not only on pottery. They inspired the Impressionists and Post-Impressionists painters as well. Monet used the high vantage point of Japanese prints with great success.

The nineteenth century became known as the Age of Imperialism. European colonization had expanded into Asia and Africa, because European nations sought cheaper labor and raw materials for their industrialization. Moreover they needed larger markets for their finished products. A resurgence of interest in the exotic developed. Chinese figures and *Des Indes* designs reappeared, this time with more accuracy. Figures wearing turbans, and exotic animals such as cockatoos, lions, elephants, and camels with howdahs, began appearing in majolica. They were well-received by consumers, both in England, on the continent, and in export markets.

The Turn of the Century

By the end of the nineteenth century a reaction to mechanization created a desire to return to a more natural lifestyle. Art Nouveau became fashionable during the late 1880s. From this movement Art Deco later developed. Some continental majolica manufacturers displayed the organic lines associated with these designs on figural pieces.

By this time majolica had become overproduced in England due in part to large orders from America; consequently, the quality declined. It was used as premiums and promotionals. Moreover, on the continent during the first part of the twentieth century hundreds of factories produced a line of majolica primarily for prizes at fairs. However, some of the leading continental manufacturers such as Sarreguemines and St. Clément continued to manufacture very fine quality products in majolica well into the twentieth century.

Chapter Two

The Union of the Arts

The Romantic Ideals

Though majolica did not appear until mid century, it is important to understand the artistic trends that developed earlier in the century because these trends influenced majolica designers. The eighteenth-century ideals reappeared in a new form as the century witnessed one revival after another. Yet the innovations of the artists brought the century to center stage artistically speaking.

Government Schools of Design originated during the 1830s and 1840s. These schools, along with the circulating exhibits at the Victoria and Albert Museum, the development of the *Art Union* and *Journal of Design and Manufacturers* magazines, and the Great Exhibition of the Industry of All Nations in London in 1851 helped create a society very much aware of stylistic trends in the decorative arts.

During the mid eighteenth century, Jean-Jacques Rousseau wrote in his *A Discourse on the Sciences and the Arts* that art must have a moral purpose, not like the art of the Rococo period which he felt damaged society. He felt that the artist had a moral obligation to paint subjects based on ancient values.

The Neo-Classical Movement, begun in the eighteenth century and based on these virtues, retained its influence throughout the nineteenth century. However, the Pre-Raphaelite Movement in England gained attention because of its rejection of the Neo-Classical style. Such artists as Dante Gabriel Rossetti used historical and spiritual inspirations for their realistic intensity. They felt art should return to Gothic and Renaissance styles.

John Ruskin, an art critic and historian, championed the cause of the Aesthetes who believed that the basis of the aesthetic feeling is morality and faith. Good art uses the beauty that God created and contributes to a good society. Bad art, on the other hand, leads to a decadent society.

Thus began the Aesthetic Movement which had its origin in England at mid century. The Aesthetes believed that life is a work of art and the intense perception of beauty is the greatest achievement. In England they began using a phrase coined by French philosopher Victor Cousin in his lectures to the Sorbonne in 1818: "art for art's sake."[1] The Pre-Raphaelite painters and the poet John Keats also helped fuel the movement with their search for intense sensation. The Aesthetic Movement gained momentum in France as well as England as the century progressed.

The Aesthetic Movement adopted the sunflower, the peacock, and the lily as its symbols. Potters of the period used these motifs to great advantage, particularly in majolica.

The Romantic Movement opposed the Neo-Classical ideals in art and pottery just as the Aesthetic Movement did. The heroic element of the classical seemed too restrictive for the emotional Romantics. The intuitive, subjective viewpoint of the Romantic contradicted the historicism of the Neo-Classical.

The Romantics reacted to the supposed rational of the Neo-Classical. The Reign of Terror after the French Revolution called into question the ability to reason, as did the Industrial Revolution with its emphasis on material goods. During the Romantic Period, the image of the solitary artist developed. Struggling with his inner conflicts, the Romantic artist saw himself as rejected by society, alone and withdrawn.

The Romantics attempted to respond to society by recreating it. Their characters increasingly separated themselves from society. The French Revolution had shifted the emphasis from society to the individual. Writers like Victor Hugo in his *Les Misérables* made the public realize that the dreams of the revolution had not materialized. Leo Tolstoy, Gustave Flaubert, and Thomas Hardy captured the attention of the public with their heroes and heroines who were outside society's norms.

The need for escape associated with the Romantic artist affected all the arts. The ballet *La Sylphide,* created by Filippo Taglioni in 1832 for his daughter, Marie, depicted a nymph who died when she could not escape the real world. The delicate, gauzy tutus and women dancing the primary roles "en pointe" established the standards for the Romantic ballet. Not until 1881 did men again returned to primary roles in ballet. *La Sylphide* affected the style of the day. Hair styles "a la sylphide" were introduced and poets as well as musicians chose spirits and fairies as subjects. Marie Taglioni became famous; Victor Hugo even wrote verses honoring her.[2]

Taglioni's delicate rendition of the nymph in *La Sylphide* made ballet a fitting subject for art. Later in the century the Impressionist artist Edgar Degas captured the labor behind the seemingly effortless art of the Romantic ballet when he painted dancers during rehearsals.

La Sylphide seemed to encapsulate the spirit of Romanticism. Death became a suitable subject for art and poetry. Pining away for love and the desire to escape the real world exemplified the ideal for the Romantic artist.

The poetry of Keats elevated longing and anticipation to an ideal. His "Ode to a Grecian Urn," a romantic interpretation of the scene on a classical vase, highlighted Romantic ideals. Anticipating an embrace yet never able to fulfill it, two lovers must endure eternity forever poised. Keats himself exemplified the Romantic persona. Even though engaged and deeply in love, he died before he could marry. Keats became the ultimate Romantic poet by never actualizing his dreams.

During this time the arts seemed to relate to each other in an unprecedented way. Frederick Chopin became the "poet of the piano." Felix Mendelssohn presented classical forms in Romantic movements, and Hector Berlioz composed the dramatic, symphonic poem. His *Symphonie fantastique* served as a "novel in tones." Franz Liszt refers to his "language of tone." Mendelssohn interpreted Shakespeare's *A Midsummer Night's Dream* musically. The fairies in the story surely appealed to the Romantics.

Georges Bizet's passionate, lyrical "drama" of *Carmen*, based on a Prosper Mérimée tale of gypsy life, failed the first night, but the notoriety caused by the subject matter helped the opera eventually to succeed with a public that loved scandal. Bizet died at thirty-seven and never knew his success. How appropriate for a Romantic composer.[3]

This interaction within the arts did not escape the pottery manufacturers. They relied upon all art forms for inspiration. Decorative arts readily displayed Romantic ideals. With the development of majolica in the last half of the century, Romantic styles resurfaced. Characters such as the jester Puck from *A Midsummer Night's Dream*, popularized musically by Mendelssohn, appeared in majolica, both by factories in England and on the continent.

Puck character jugs became very popular perhaps because of interest in performances of *A Midsummer Night's Dream*. Sarreguemines manufactured this Puck jug, but companies in England and Germany made similar ones in pottery, porcelain, and lusterware. $100-150

The Realists

In the 1840s Charles Baudelaire, the French poet, encouraged the artist to oppose historicism and to appreciate the heroism of everyday life and contemporary society. The uniqueness of the individual ruled supreme. Gustave Gourbet's paintings of everyday scenes defied the conventional wisdom that common people were not fit subjects for art. The public scandal surrounding his painting *The Bathers* with its nudes did a great deal to attract attention to the arts in a society that endorsed sensationalism.

The second half of the nineteenth century witnessed a great deal of progress in science and industry. Emphasis on reality opposed the Romantic individualism. The Romantics had interpreted nature, not just captured it. They created mythical landscapes of their own, unlike the Realists who preferred actual representations of it. The artists of the time had access to scholarship through the libraries, so dramatic versions of current events appeared.

The invention of the camera aided the developing appreciation of reality. The middle class appreciated art and music as entertainment, but they also appreciated the scientific advancements of their era. The idealization and sentimentalization of the medieval past that had so attracted the Romantics contrasted with the Realists' view of the world. The Realists studied society and attitudes in an analytical, not an emotional, way.

Writers such as Émile Zola and Charles Dickens scrutinized society. They portrayed working class individuals struggling merely to survive. The public loved the characters of Dickens, and he became the first literary celebrity. Because all of Dickens' works originally appeared in magazine installments, he is credited with inventing the serial novel. An unbelievable 81% of literate people bought a copy of *The Pickwick Papers*, setting a record that still stands.[4]

Figures of Dickens' characters appeared on the market. A Staffordshire toby jug of Mr. Pickwick which, though not majolica, possibly encouraged majolica designers to consider contemporary fictional characters and issues as subjects for tobies. Earthenware and parian examples of military heroes and royalty displayed a serious air. Shakespeare's comedic characters appeared as toby jugs, but humorous treatments of contemporary political figures were elevated to an art form in turn of the century French majolica figural production.

This Staffordshire toby jug of the popular Charles Dickens' character Mr. Pickwick was probably one of the first jugs in the shape of a contemporary fictional figure, perhaps establishing the precedent for later toby jugs. Earlier tobies modeled after Shakespearean characters or historical figures (as well as stereotypical figures) were popular, but few offered characters from contemporary society. NP

The use of everyday life as subjects for art and literature strongly influenced the pottery manufacturers at the end of the nineteenth century. Manufacturers of majolica figures treated public scandals with humor. Fashion trends appeared in pottery. Political figures acquired fame or stung from ridicule, depending upon the attitude of the potter, when they became a toby jug. The decorative arts no longer distanced themselves from the average consumer.

The Impressionists

Just before 1860 the Impressionist Movement began. The painter tried to convey reality through the use of details and textures. He gave an "impression" of reality, an essence of reality. Impressionists concerned themselves with the effects of sunlight and an increased color range. Their landscapes relied upon imagination, not reality.

The Impressionists painted the bourgeois in everyday life. The middle class enjoying parks, outings, and recreation attracted the attention of painters like Monet and Renoir. Pissaro, Degas, and Manet painted everyday life without pretense.

The Impressionists concerned themselves with figures: Manet wanted to study the figure in the natural environment, Degas used figures in action, and Renoir studied women and children with their delicate qualities. Renoir perhaps discovered his trademark use of ivory and pinks

while working as a porcelain decorator. His subjects have a pearl-like appearance reminiscent of fine porcelain.

The Impressionists exhibited their art in group exhibits rather than the Salon exhibits. The Salon had begun in the eighteenth century as a way of directing public tastes. Now the Impressionists defied the restrictions of society and created their own shows, thus changing the relationship between the artist and his public.

This willingness to defy the rules, reminiscent of the Romantics, also typified Victorian society. It seemed eager to expand its horizons and accepted creativity and individuality. Majolica manufacturers used this attitude to their advantage, creating strikingly different pieces of pottery. The Impressionists' interest in figures may have attracted the attention of majolica manufacturers, for numerous figures appeared on the market both in England and on the continent. For thousands of years artists had crafted figural designs of royalty and animals, but the use of everyday people as subjects for the artist came of age with the Impressionists.

The Post-Impressionists

After the Franco-Prussian War ended in 1871, the Impressionist group separated and went their own ways artistically. The attitude of painters toward color was changing as they realized the impossibility of capturing nature on canvas.

Post-Impressionists wanted to express feelings rather than reality. The 1880s saw an experimental trend with painters like Cézanne, Gauguin, Van Gogh, and Matisse. Cézanne tried to capture sunlight through use of color. His concern, like that of other Post-Impressionists, for the effects of color perhaps influenced potters like the Massiers in the south of France. The Massiers experimented with colors and developed new, brightly colored glazes for their majolica figures, colors reminiscent of the Post-Impressionists: ochre, cadmium red, ultramarine and cobalt blue, raw sienna, burnt umber, and chartreuse.

The Post-Impressionists acknowledged music as a creative influence. Cézanne's *Overture to Tannhäuser* indicated the artist's awareness of the intertwined arts. Painters like Whistler, though not included in this group but strongly influenced by the Impressionists, entitled several of his paintings after musical terms: *Symphony in White, Arrangement in Gray and Black, and Nocturnes.*

Musicians like Claude Debussy, on the other hand, tried to use the subtlety of the Impressionists paintings to write symphonies. Antonin Dvorák used the German romanticism and love of folklore as his inspiration for music with an ethnic overtone.

Musicians wanted to add poetry while poets wanted music to go with their verse. Debussy composed *Prélude à l'après-midi d'un faune* after a story by Stéphane Mallarmé. Nijinsky, the famed dancer, later appeared in Paris performing the principal role in the ballet of the same

name. Strauss incorporated the sounds of nature and animals in his tone poems. The German composer Richard Wagner used musical symbols to represent a person or theme much like poets used symbolism. His works relied heavily on the dramatic and had a wide appeal in France where Sunday afternoon "popular concerts" featured his music. Poets, too, fell under the spell of relying upon other art forms for inspiration. Rimbaud gave each vowel a color: A black, E white, I red, O blue, U green. He tried to invent a poetic language much as an artist created a painting.[5]

Many artists worked in more than one medium. Both Paul Gauguin and Pablo Picasso expressed themselves on canvas and in clay. Paul Gauguin, a friend of Ernest Chaplet who had joined the Choisy-le-Roi pottery factory in 1887, made bright stoneware which Chaplet fired for him.[6] Choisy was a leading majolica manufacturer. Picasso, also an artist and potter, lived and worked in Vallauris, France, the home of the Massier pottery firm. Both Picasso and the Massiers sought to stretch the limits of ceramics, each

Choisy-le-Roi made some very fine majolica, especially florals, but this rooster planter is one of the few Choisy figurals. Compare the cadmium red and raw sienna colors of this piece with some of the Impressionists paintings. 15" high. $2,000-2,500

in his own way: Picasso with his modernistic designs and the Massiers with their revolutionary colors for majolica.

Oscar Wilde once said, "art imitates life." Perhaps this was never more true than with the pottery figures of the period. It was during this period that many of the majolica factories, particularly in France, were making toby jugs and figural pitchers. The range of tobies included political personages, humorous treatments of current events, and representations of historical events in the form of people. Onnaing potters, in particular, treated contemporary issues with humor.

Art Nouveau

John Ruskin had sought a return to true craftsmanship rather than mass produced goods in an effort to find true beauty. In 1861 painter William Morris, a friend of Ruskin, founded Morris & Company to enable a craftsman to practice his art rather than work at factory labor. He wanted the skilled laborers to feel pride in their accomplishments, and he wanted the average home to appreciate true beauty, not mass production.

Morris & Company combined the skills of artists, craftsman, and architects. For the first time a collaboration of the arts presented itself. Morris hired many of the Pre-Raphaelite painters like Rossetti and Edward Burne-Jones to decorate furniture, as he appreciated their idealized view of the Middle Ages.

The Morris style, however, used natural forms as a source for design much the same as the designers of the Middle Ages did. This harmony of effort and use of organic lines foreshadowed the shapes of Art Nouveau.

In 1888 Morris founded the Arts and Crafts Society because he felt that laborers should gain pleasure from their efforts and not be forced to toil in a factory. He also believed that society could achieve reform through craftsmanship. Hand produced goods, including furniture, floor coverings, and decorative arts reminiscent of Gothic patterns appeared on the market. Even though these goods remained too expensive for the average consumer, the Arts and Crafts movement had begun.

Another proponent of the Arts and Crafts ideals was Arthur Mackmurdo. Both Morris and Mackmurdo based their designs on natural sources, but the free-flowing lines of Art Nouveau first appeared in works by the Century Guild established by Mackmurdo in 1884. Art Nouveau encompassed all of the arts much like Morris' concept.

The combination of curves, delicate patterns, and the overall lightness of Art Nouveau appealed to the Victorians as well as the continental Europeans of the nineteenth century. The style was exhibited at the 1889 and 1900 Universal Exhibitions in Paris. Organic elements derived from nature and not from history appeared as designers returned to a fundamental approach. This approach rejected the revivalism of the past century.

Music and literature also served as inspiration for Art Nouveau just as it had for the Impressionists. Émile Gallé tried to give his work added significance by inscribing quotations or poems on his furniture and glassware.

The public accepted the graphic arts of the Art Nouveau as equal to painting. The leading graphic artist was Henri de Toulouse-Lautrec who rose to fame painting cabaret scenes. The curving lines and flat shapes of his posters became commonplace after the French law of 1881 gave liberty to the press.[7] Although posters began in the 1830s, it was not until the end of the century that the advertisements with bright illustrations captured the attention of the public.

Twentieth Century Modernism

The twentieth century began on a modern note in all art forms. After the turn of the century dancers like Isadora Duncan improvised free flowing movements to music by Camille Saint-Saëns. Duncan became the leader of the modern dance revolution which spread rapidly. Modern dance stressed freedom from the restrictive, unnatural structure of balletic movements and emphasized emotional responses perhaps influenced by the Post-Impressionists and their emphasis on feelings. No longer did dancers wear the tight bodices of romantic tutus, but instead wore loose, breezy garments.

Art, too, was transforming. Cézanne's spatial forms led to the geometrical style of the Cubists like Picasso and Braque. Van Gogh's emotional emphasis and Gauguin's freedom led to the development of Fauvism. Matisse's style evolved, and he became a leading proponent of Fauvism. Both of these movements stressed expressive use of color and line to create the illusion of three dimensions. The last two decades of the nineteenth century witnessed a trend toward experimentation in the arts, and this willingness to try something new affected the pottery manufacturers. New figures, some well-received and some not, emerged.

The emphasis on intense color and more abstract lines with fewer restrictions translated to the majolica of the twentieth century. A freer line and an expanded range of colors evolved. As mentioned, by this time consumer interest in majolica diminished in part due to overproduction. Since production had begun earlier in England, it follows that decline in consumer interest would initiate there. Perhaps the Victorian love of change, as well as overproduction, caused consumers to turn their attention elsewhere. On the continent, however, production continued. In addition to the major majolica manufacturers who continued to produce high quality majolica, cottage industries abounded.

With the interest in colors towards the end of the nineteenth century and the early part of the twentieth, majolica producers sought a greater diversity in color. Brighter faces on toby jugs and more unusual colors on figures appeared. Lemon yellows, golden browns, and chartreuses emerged on figures.

Though majolica is still being produced today, much of the figural production relies on reproducing models popularized by the nineteenth century manufacturers. While a testament to the creative genius of the original producers and designers, these reproductions lack the subtlety and delicate detail of the originals.

Collecting majolica figures develops an awareness of the century, the society, and the arts of the nineteenth and early twentieth centuries. By studying the artistic developments, one sees how these advancements affected pottery production. The collector acquires a deeper appreciation not only for the pottery, but for the ingenuity of the designers.

Chapter Three

English Firms: Major Manufacturers

Minton: The Creator of Majolica

Born in 1765, Thomas Minton apprenticed to Josiah Spode as an engraver. It was there that he created the famous Blue Willow pattern. By 1793 Minton decided that he wanted to open his own firm and acquired land containing clay and tin mines in Stoke-on-Trent. Llewellynn Jewitt, author of *The Ceramic Art of Great Britain* first published in 1878, describes the Minton site as having one "bisque" kiln and one "glost" kiln as well as a "sliphouse for preparing the clay" and a few other buildings (rev. ed. 1883, p. 396).

Minton acquired a partner, Joseph Poulson, a potter whose brother Samuel acted as a modeler and mold-maker. In May of 1796 the firm opened. Minton's brother Arthur served as trade agent. William Pownall, a Liverpool merchant financed part of the enterprise and was a silent partner for a few years. The name of the firm became Minton, Poulson, and Pownall until Poulson's death in 1808.

Minton and his primary competitor, Copeland, vied for market share over parian. Discovered at Copeland while trying to rediscover the old Derby biscuit formula with a former Derby employee, "statuary porcelain" was considered extremely suitable for figures. According to Jewitt, Thomas took out a patent in 1839 for his "parian," an "improved porcelain" consisting of "Kaolin or Cornish clay, made into cream and passed through sieves; Dorsetshire or similar clay treated in like manner; and pure feldspar, all in certain proportions and mixed with great care" (p. 399).

Soon many firms produced parian figures. Victorians responded to the marble like appearance, and numerous households boasted parian statuettes which were copies of ancient marble statues.

By 1817 Minton's sons Thomas and Herbert had become partners and the firm became "Thomas Minton and Sons." By 1836 Herbert took control and the Minton firm was the largest in the area. The Minton family's collection of French Sèvres and Chinese hard-paste porcelains served as inspiration for many of the pottery designs. Minton's parrot on a pierced rock closely resembles the Kangxin porcelain parrot of the seventeenth century. The Chinese parrot has reds, greens, and purples while Minton's has a deep blue-green color. Minton's cockatoo, however, displays the reds and greens of the Chinese parrot.

Turquoise, an old color in glazes which covered the Persian wares from the twelfth century, also highlighted the Chinese wares like the Ming of the late sixteenth century. These wares had colored floral decoration on a turquoise ground. Sèvres used both turquoise and cobalt blues, colors with which Minton majolica is often associated. Other inspirations for majolica include the Palissy collection of the Duke of Sutherland, Minton's mentor.

In 1848 Émile Jeannest, a Frenchman, became the first of many French designers to work for Minton. Jeannest began a modeling school which Minton helped sponsor called the Potteries School of Design. The year of 1849 was monumental for Minton. He met his friend, Henry Cole, in Paris. During this trip, Cole visited the Denière ornamentalists where Albert-Ernest Carrier-Belleuse worked, whom Minton later recruited. Following his work at Minton, Carrier-Belleuse, who had also worked for Wedgwood, returned to France to become Art Director for Sèvres. In addition, he modeled for Choisy-le-Roi. Minton, however, maintained contact with him and held exclusive English rights to his designs. In the same year the co-director of Manufacture Valentine at Saint-Gaudens, Joseph-Léon-François Arnoux, was recruited by Minton. Family connections between Minton and Arnoux and visits to Arnoux by Minton prior to that year indicate that perhaps Minton already had plans to incorporate more French designers.[1]

Arnoux, who had studied pottery at the Royal Manufactory of Sèvres, accepted Minton's offer of becoming Art Director, perhaps in part due to the revolution of workers in 1848 in France. It was Arnoux who developed the kilns and glazes necessary for majolica. His Patent Oven allowed for more space and better heating distribution and his glazes gave majolica their lustrous appeal.[2]

Perhaps the revival of interest in classical figures created a market that soon would witness innovative figures in majolica, not just parian. In 1849 the Minton trade books carried "Majolica," though it was not until the Great Exhibition in 1851 that it created a public sensation.

Developed in an attempt to recreate *maiolica*, the Hispano-Moresque pottery imported into Italy via the island of Majorca, Minton anglicized the name. Its public introduction at the Great Exhibition attracted enormous attention. This cane-colored earthenware covered with a tin-enamel glaze captured the attention of the consuming public. Minton majolica, according to Jewitt, is known for its "sharpness of details, purity of colours, excellence of glaze, and artistic character" (p.402).

The exhibition, often called the first World's Fair, offered exhibits from industrialized nations. Great Britain used one half of the space, while other industrialized nations exhibited in the other half. Between May 1 and October 11 over 6 million people visited the Crystal Palace where almost 14,000 firms were represented.[3] Since the exhibition was organized to showcase new technology and decorative arts, it was fitting that part of the proceeds go to support the Victoria and Albert Museum Foundation. The museum established by example the standards of design for the decorative arts.

Judges awarded prizes for unique, inventive, and technically skilled offerings. Minton won a coveted award at this exhibition, and at every other exhibition both domestic and foreign in the following years.

By 1869 critics began to feel that majolica relied too heavily upon imitation:

> The art of Majolica . . . can no longer
> content itself with the mere reproduction
> of pieces, even of the finest specimens of
> Italian art. . . . It must transform itself as
> all other arts have done.[4]

Minton took the critics seriously and soon began creating more imaginative pieces. No longer relying upon the use of the old parian molds, Minton sought new and innovative designs. He began making figures from original molds.

This list, provided by Joan Jones, Curator for the Minton Museum, Royal Doulton PLC, indicates the numbered Minton figures with majolica glazes, though it does not include ornamentals. Minton made 505 figures, but not all were manufactured in majolica.

75 Easy Johnny (nodding figure)
81 Coachee (nodding figure)
187 Infant Neptune by H J Townsend
224 Angel Font by J Bell
257 Children with Goat
258 Children with Goat
280 Boy with oval basket for matches by Carrier
281 Girl with oval basket for matches by Carrier
282 Boy with bamboo basket by Carrier
283 Girl with bamboo basket by Carrier
286 French horse
291 Monkey Musician by Carrier
292 Monkey Musician by Carrier (companion to 291)
293 Hogarth Match Boy by Carrier
294 Hogarth Match Girl by Carrier

296 The Vintagers by Carrier
312 Grape Bearer by Carrier
313 Grape Bearer by Carrier (companion to 312)
318 Double Cupid Salt
326 Sea Horse with Shell by Carrier
327 Cain and Abel by Carrier
329 Adam by Carrier
330 Eve by Carrier
361 Boy and Donkey
365 Vintagers with shell, after Carrier
367 Science by Carrier
368 Art by Carrier
370 Knitting Girl by Mrs. Thornycroft
371 Shipping Girl by Mrs. Thornycroft
373 Cupid & Basket
375 Vintager with Basket before and behind by Protât
376 Vintager with Basket in each hand by Protât
383 Lady Godiva by J Thomas
395 Boy with Staghound on oval pedestal by Jeannest
396 Boy & Stag on pedestal by Jeannest
397 Literature by Birks
401 Fishing by Jeannest
403 Boy & Foxhound by Jeannest
404 Boy & Fox by Jeannest
405 Vintager with Basket by Carrier
406 Vintager with Basket by Carrier
407 Cupid with Basket by Carrier
409 Chickens by J Bell
413 Man with Wheelbarrow by J B Klagmann
416 Crossing Sweeper by C Abbot
417 Orange Girl by C Abbot
421 Boy Resting on Basket
424 Vintagers
431 Girl Resting on Basket (companion to 421)
432 Boy & Shell
433 Girl & Shell
437 Cupid with Shell
449 Donkey with Panniers
460 Cupid Flower Holder
463 The Reader Flower Holder by Carrier
466 Vintager
475 Savoyard
476 Cupid & Shell

Perhaps one of the most famous of Minton's animals is the ornamental Paul Comolera peacock (no. 2045). While being shipped to the International Exhibition in Melbourne in 1880, the ship called the *Loch Ard* capsized near Warrnambool, Australia. The crate containing the peacock, appropriately enough a symbol of survival and resurrection, washed ashore and was salvaged. After passing through several hands, the peacock is now on exhibit at the Warrnambool Flagstaff Hill Memorial Village in Australia.[5]

When Herbert Minton died in 1858 the Minton firm was one of the largest, producing some of the most innovative products of the time. One year later Herbert's nephew and partner, Michael Daintry Hollins, took over direction of the factory. By 1875 the plant boasted 1,500 employees including 200 enamelers from Europe.[6] Majolica perhaps had served to increase the popularity of Minton, but by the 1880s majolica had become so common that it was no longer desirable for the upper middle class. An article in *The Pottery Gazette* of 1882 stated that:

> The Majolica makers are taking alarm. The trade is going to the bad; prices are so low that profits are next to nil. Almost every article in domestic use is now made in Majolica. . . . The only fault perhaps is that it has become common.[7]

By 1890 the new style of Art Nouveau began to appear in the decorative arts, although the style appeared more on continental majolica than English majolica. In England majolica was no longer considered stylish except for conservatories. Following the Philadelphia Centennial Exhibition in 1876, the American market eagerly imported majolica from the 130 English manufacturers. However, this market was not enough to save the majolica manufacturers. The combination of overproduction, cheaper imitations, and new laws regulating the lead content of glazes lead to the decline of English majolica.

Minton had displayed his famous majolica at numerous exhibitions. He had participated in the London International Exhibition of 1862, the South Kensington Exhibition of 1871, the Paris Exhibition in 1867, and the United States Centennial Exhibition of 1876. At the Vienna Exhibition of 1873, majolica still retained its popularity: only 64 items of the 549 taken to exhibit returned unsold at the close of the exhibit. In 1878 Colin Minton Campbell, nephew of Herbert, received the Legion d'Honneur at the Paris Exhibition. Minton also displayed majolica at the Sydney Exhibition of 1879 and the Paris Exhibitions of 1889, which the introduction of the Eiffel Tower made famous, and 1900. In 1894 majolica was displayed for the last time publicly at the Imperial Institute Exhibition of Pottery and Glass in London.[8]

Marks on Minton included the impressed name in all capital letters. Later the mark appeared in ink. The "s" was added after the name in 1872. Date codes also appear.

MINTON

Animals in Design

Since ancient times man has made images of himself or his animals in earthenware. The scientific advancements of the nineteenth century perhaps served to revitalize interest in many of these figures. In addition, interest in the exotic tales of travelers inspired pottery designers to include uncommon animals as a part of the overall design.

As early as 1900 B.C. earthenware figures were used as tomb furnishings in Egypt. Such animals as dogs, fox, monkeys, and apes were enclosed to insure the safe and efficient transport of the spirit to the next realm. Earthenware figures of realistic monkeys appeared as finials for staffs around 750. B.C. Other figures include the hippopotamus and the crocodile which were hunted in the Nile. Earthenware camels, pigs, and cows as well as the ibex (which resembles a deer) have been discovered as early as 600 B.C. in Egypt.

In ancient China camels and horses laden for trade were important tomb furnishings. As early as the second century B.C. pottery figures resembling these animals, either stationary or braying, indicate the relative significance of them in the daily lives of the people. Chinese tomb figures included earthenware rhinoceroses with a greenish color resulting from a lead glaze colored with copper. These date from the Han Dynasty, 206 B.C. to A.D. 220.

Also in ancient China the Dogs of Fo, which resembled lions, protected the palace by warding off evil spirits. First made in simple earthenware and later with a turquoise glaze, these dogs had manes like a lion, but lions are not indigenous to China.

The Chavin people of the Central Andes worshipped a god in the shape of a cat as early as 800 B.C. Mice also appeared in pottery design at about the same time.[9]

Since every Victorian lady was judged by her gentility, it is easy to see why dogs and cats became favorite subjects for Victorians. Gentleness towards these animals, especially the dog, indicated class. One need only examine the portraiture and paintings of the period to notice the abundance of women with children and dogs.

Meissen examples of animals in the early eighteenth century seemed to serve as inspiration for Minton and his followers. Many of the Meissen figures exhibit animals in action. While Minton's animals seem regal and contemplative, those of his follower George Jones often capture creatures in the midst of a step or flight.

The Victorian interest in natural history encouraged the South Kensington Museum, later called the Victoria

Minton monkey garden seat. Circa 1860. 18.25" high. (Beware-Unmarked reproductions exist in a slightly smaller size.) *Courtesy of William Doyle Galleries Auctioneers & Appraisers* $12,000-16,000

and Albert, and other museums to establish exhibits showcasing new discoveries in archaeology and other sciences. Since the nineteenth-century middle class enjoyed visits to museums, it is entirely likely that many of the exhibits inspired the wonderfully creative genius of the contemporary pottery designers.

Deer are ancient Mongolian figural designs dating from the fifth to third century B.C. A bronze finial of a deer head from this time period is on exhibit at the Victoria and Albert Museum in London. Other exhibits include the alkaline turquoise glaze with tin-oxide pottery from twelfth- or early thirteenth-century Persia. A water vessel in the shape of a lion appears similar to later pottery figures.

The heads of Boar appeared as tureens in the seventeenth-century in faïence and served as inspiration for many of the French manufacturers of majolica. Witness the tureen by Sarreguemines that closely resembles the eighteenth-century faïence one found in the Musée de Saint-Omer in France.

Exotic animals like the elephant and water buffalo appeared in pottery. In the eighteenth century Ralph Wood and Thomas Whieldon manufactured figures in these shapes. A century later similar animals, along with other atypical creatures, appeared on the majolica market. Jungle animals became popular figures again.

Chickens commonly appeared in majolica not only in France, but in England as well. Since it is the national symbol for France just as Uncle Sam is for the United States and John Bull is for England, numerous majolica chickens appeared from a variety of firms in France. However, firms in England included chickens in their designs like the Minton cockerel teapot and the cockerel and hen spill vases. George Jones included a hen teapot in his figures.

Other food sources besides the chicken maintained their popularity through the centuries as designs in pottery. Cows and pigs numbered high on the majolica designers' list of favorites. Charming frogs and fish enticed consumers into buying them. Game dishes appealed to the landed gentry.

A Minton figural cat holding a mouse under its paw. 9.5" high. *Photography by Jill Graham* $5,000-6,000

John Henk also modeled this life size stork (no. 1916). Circa 1870.
Courtesy of Minton Museum. Royal Doulton PLC

Similar designs sometimes appeared both as decoration and as
figurals. This Minton giant heron flower stand modeled by John
Henk is 39" high (no. 1917). Joseph Holdcroft as well as potters on
the continent later copied these designs. Circa 1876. *Courtesy of
William Doyle Galleries Auctioneers & Appraisers* $12,000-16,000

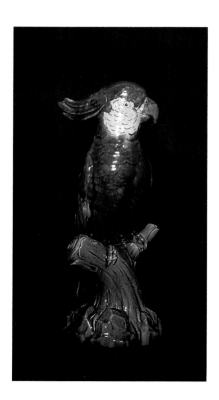

Birds of all sorts were popular designs for figurals in the nineteenth century, both in England and on the Continent. This Minton cockatoo somewhat resembles a Meissen figurine made earlier in the century. 12.5" high. Minton frequently used Meissen designs for inspiration. $600-1,000

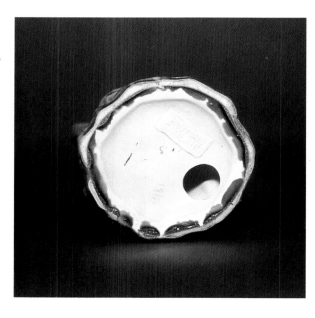

The Mintons mark dates this piece from 1890-1910.

A Minton frog riding a Renaissance style dolphin illustrates the whimsy of Victorian majolica figurals. *Photography by Jill Graham* $4,500-5,500

Minton frog on a box designed to look like rocks. 4" high. $4,000-4,500

Two charming Minton begging dogs as condiment dishes. Dogs have been one of the most popular figures used in pottery design.

Earthenware dogs have been found in Ancient Egyptian tombs dating from 1900 B.C. Respective heights 2" and 6". $2,000-2,500

Cockerel (no. 1982) and Hen (no. 1983) spill vases modeled by John Henk. Circa 1876. 13" and 12" respectively. *Courtesy of Minton Museum, Royal Doulton PLC*

The Minton clinging monkey teapot was one of many designs imitated by French potters. As no copyright laws existed factories openly copied popular designs of another factory. 6.5" high. $3,000-4,400

The Aesthetic Movement which began in the 1850s used the peacock as one of its symbols. This Minton peacock certainly captures the sentiments of the movement. Minton peacock (no. 2045) modeled by Paul Comolera. Circa 1873. 62" high. *Courtesy of Minton Museum, Royal Doulton PLC*

Besides domesticated animals, jungle animals, and food sources, other majolica figures included a variety of birds from the eagle and cockatoo to the wren. Few animals escaped the attention of the majolica designers.

Human Figures in Design

Pottery is one of the oldest of the art forms. One need only water, clay, and sun. It was only natural that ancient man would enjoy capturing his image in clay, just as he drew his image on the walls of caves. Human figures have evolved over the centuries, becoming less stylized. Eventually human figures depicted accurate musculature and proportion.

By the nineteenth century majolica designers had exposure not only to ancient Greek artistry but also to Renaissance paintings. These figures in motion perhaps inspired manufacturers like Minton to duplicate the action. Though Minton's animals often appear statuesque and stately, many of his human figures seem to be caught in action like a candid snapshot. They appear quite realistic. Witness the man and the wheelbarrow in mid-step or the posy holders with their arms aloft. Both seem in the midst of motion.

Many of the English majolica manufacturers used *putti* as designs on pottery because of the popularity of the Renaissance Revival and later because of the popularity of the "French Antique" styles. Examples of *putti* figures are included, but as they were numerous, it is impossible to include figures by every manufacturer. After giving several examples, only mention will be made that the manufacturers included *putti* figurals in their production. Often the English factories with limited productions of human figures used putti almost exclusively. With the exception of Minton, it seems that greater variety existed in English figural productions of animals, while the opposite appears true of the French productions. Moreover, continental productions also seem to have more variety in their human figural production.

An extremely rare Minton garden seat depicting a well-modeled child holding a pillow. Rare

Close-ups showing details of the Minton garden seat. Note the upturned toes inside the shoes and the realistic detail of the fur and claws. The fur probably required a special glaze.

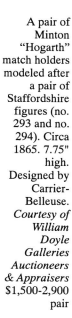

A pair of Minton "Hogarth" match holders modeled after a pair of Staffordshire figures (no. 293 and no. 294). Circa 1865. 7.75" high. Designed by Carrier-Belleuse. *Courtesy of William Doyle Galleries Auctioneers & Appraisers* $1,500-2,900 pair

The companion piece to the garden seat. This child faces the opposite direction.

Minton "posy holders" designed as peasants with baskets for matches. Circa 1870. 8.25" high. *Courtesy of William Doyle Galleries Auctioneers & Appraisers* $2,000-3,200 pair

A Minton figural serving dish on the right in the shape of a mermaid whose tail forms the handle. Circa 1870. 8" long. On the left is a George Jones figural salt shaped as a putto on a shell supported by a dolphin. 7.5" high. *Courtesy of William Doyle Galleries Auctioneers & Appraisers* $1,200-1,600 Minton; $900-1,350 Jones

This wonderful statuette of a woman depicts the well known cobalt blue used with distinction on Minton majolica. 14.25" high. *Photography by Jill Graham* $4,000-5,000

Although unmarked, this *putto* (one of a pair) riding a goat is attributed to Minton, designed after a model by Meissen. Holdcroft made a similar figure. Circa 1870. 9" high. *Courtesy of William Doyle Galleries Auctioneers & Appraisers* $750-1,100

The man with the wheelbarrow figural modeled by Klagmann for Minton in 1864 typifies the quality of design and coloring of the manufacturer's figurals (no. 413). 13.25" high by 11" long. *Courtesy of Minton Museum, Royal Doulton PLC*

According to Minton pattern books this jug is listed as a "male in eighteenth century dress," but it is commonly referred to as the Barrister (no. 1140). The companion piece is referred to as the Lady (no. 1139). Circa 1865. Both 11" high. *Photography by Jill Graham* $2,000-2,500

George Jones

Though few factory records remain, some history of the factory is available. George Jones established the Trent Pottery in 1861 in Stoke-on-Trent after a twelve year apprenticeship at Minton. Jones was forty-seven years old according to the 1871 census, and his factory had 570 workers. The firm began with the production of parian, but eventually became most well-known for its "rustic" majolica. Jones exhibited in Paris in 1867, London in 1871, Vienna in 1873, and Sydney in 1876 where he gained coveted medals. In 1873 Jones was joined by his three sons: Frank Jones-Benham, a potter; Horace O. Jones who had studied art at South Kensington and became director of the designs; and George H. Jones who handled the sales and financial department. The firm's monogrammed mark added "& Sons." Another partner, W. Candland, remained until his death in 1902. George died at the end of 1893, and the three sons along with Candland continued to manage the business.[10]

Jones specialized in majolica and it is highly collectible today. His animals exhibit intense motion and draw the observer into the action. The color and attention to detail reflect the Minton apprenticeship, but the intense action of many of the animal figures remains distinctly Jones. Many of the Jones figures are marked, but even unmarked pieces have a tell-tale reserved white space with a pattern number and letter (possibly for the decorator) in the mottled green and brown underside.

George Jones majolica, according to Jewitt, is "of a high order of art" (p. 418). Renamed the Crescent Pottery in 1893, the firm closed in 1951.

An extremely rare tortoise spittoon by George Jones. Many experts believed that this piece is one of a very few ever manufactured. The removable shell acts as a cover for the receptacle. (no. 3331). Circa 1873. Rare

Many of the George Jones figurals exhibit intense motion as if caught in the middle of an action. This eagle appears to take flight. Note the wonderful detail of the feathers on this wall mount. $900-1,100

A George Jones teapot showing a hen (sometimes called a cockerel) poised in mid-step, unlike a similar one by Minton. Circa 1876. 11" long. *Courtesy of Majolica Auctions by Michael G. Strawser* $3,500-5,000

Two George Jones birds on nests. The smaller nest is a box while the larger with a wren carefully perched on the side holds place cards. Circa 1874. Wren (no. 3384). $1,500-2,000 box; $2,500-3,500 card holder

Part of a smoking set by George Jones, this ashtray has a cat struggling to hold onto it somewhat reminiscent of the Minton dog on the edge of his bowl. Similar Jones ashtrays depicted a dog or fox. Circa 1880. *Britannia, Grays Antique Market, London* $1,000-1,500

George Jones manufactured a series of fox and hound centerpieces. The action of the hunting dog contrasts nicely with the stately pose of the deer. Circa 1879. $4,000-5,000

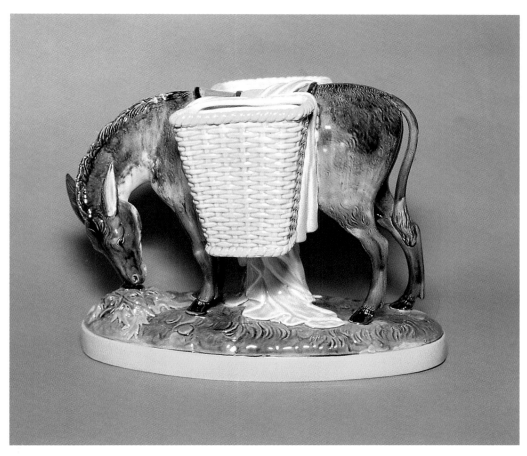

These burro and camel (no. 2782) sweetmeat dishes by George Jones date from 1868. $4,500-5,500 burro; $5,500-6,500 camel

Holidays were special occasions as indicated by the unusual George Jones "Punch" bowl made for the Christmas season and decorated with holly. Punch was a popular figure both with children and adults, so this recumbent figure of him must have had a broad appeal. Circa 1878. 11" diameter. *Britannia, Grays Antique Market, London* $7,000-9,000

A George Jones centerpiece depicting Neptune straddling a water-spewing Renaissance style dolphin (no. 3262), 15.5" high. The companion piece (not shown here) is a female sea nymph. *Britannia, Grays Antique Market, London* $4,000-5,000

Close-up of Neptune's face.

A variety of *putti* figurals, most by George Jones, accompany this Copeland "Sloth and Mischief" figure. Since the figure is marked "depose," the piece was probably decorated in France. Circa 1885. 17.25" high. *Courtesy of William Doyle Galleries Auctioneers & Appraisers* $4,000-6,000

A pair of Copeland candleholders showing a boy with his dog and a girl carrying a lamb. Circa 1870. 10.75" high. *Courtesy of William Doyle Galleries Auctioneers & Appraisers* $2,500-5,000

A Minton match holder, circa 1868, 7.75" high is on the left. Center is a Copeland parian piece with a majolica glaze. Circa 1880. 7" high. Right is an unattributed *putti* 7.5" high. *Courtesy of William Doyle Galleries Auctioneers & Appraisers* $800-1,200 Minton and Copeland; $150-250 unattributed

In 1833 William Taylor Copeland bought the Spode firm begun by Josiah Spode in Stoke-on-Trent in 1770. Spode had developed a reputation for fine blue and white transfer-printed ware. Copeland took his sons into partnership in 1867, and the firm's name became W. T. Copeland & Sons. Although known for parian and bone china, the company also continued the production of transfer-print wares.

Copeland made majolica in the 1870s, though much of the figural production centered on Renaissance Revival *putti* pieces. Included in this chapter because of the excellent quality of their figures, Copeland majolica is often grouped with Minton, Jones, or Holdcroft in auction catalogs. Copeland majolica or majolica-glazed products have nice detailing and fine modeling. The body of the figures is somewhat lighter in color than other majolica. Copeland advertised widely and exhibited at the Centennial Exhibition in Philadelphia in 1876 along with other international exhibitions. The firm enjoyed a prestigious reputation and royal patronage.

In addition to *putti* figural pieces Copeland also made a seated Mandarin milk jug indicating an awareness of the revival of interest in *Chinoiserie*, and the wonderful "Sloth & Mischief" figure which depicts a long-haired monkey riding a tortoise. Copeland also manufactured shepherd figural pieces.

Most Copeland majolica is marked with the impressed name in all capital letters followed by the British registry mark or a two digit number indicating the year. The firm is still in production.

Little is known about the Holdcroft firm except that Holdcroft established his Sutherland Pottery factory at Daisy Bank in Longton in 1870. Jewitt seemed impressed with Holdcroft's wares as she writes that "his productions rank deservedly high" (p. 550). Holdcroft marketed his products to the continent, Australia, and South America.

Holdcroft had been apprenticed to Minton for eighteen years and his figures reflect a similarity of design. Note the stork and heron flower stands. Majolica helped Holdcroft establish his reputation. *The Pottery & Glass Trades' Review* of October 1878 notes:

> . . . the effect [of the stork and heron flower stands] is very fine. That this manufactory turns out good majolica work is evidenced by the fact that during all the late bad times, Mr. Holdcroft has been quite busy in executing orders from Paris, Rome, Naples, and other such places where a pretty thing is known when seen, and an ugly thing likewise.[11]

However, not everyone agrees. Some contemporary critics feel that Holdcroft majolica lacks the accuracy, artistry, and novelty that Minton's majolica exhibited.[12]

The firm became Holdcroft's Limited in 1906 and in 1920 the factory closed. Majolica wares are marked with a monogram alone or within a circle. Much Holdcroft majolica has a celadon green underside, but other colors include gray, brown, black, or a mottled combination of the last two.

Holdcroft flower stands resemble the Minton examples. The stork with the snake is 31.25" tall while the stork with the minnow is 29" tall. Circa 1875. *Courtesy of William Doyle Galleries Auctioneers & Appraisers* $6,000-9,000

This duck relaxing on a leaf is a Holdcroft preserves pot. *Britannia, Grays Antique Market, London* $1,200-1,600

Compare this rooster which was probably made by Holdcroft to the one by Choisy and the one by Minton. The similar use of colors perhaps speaks to the influence of Impressionist art with its raw siennas, burnt umbers, and cadmium reds. *Britannia, Grays Antique Market, London* $1,700-2,300

The popularity of Renaissance styled dolphins in Victorian England was widespread. These Holdcroft examples intertwine to hold a shell bowl aloft. Circa 1875. 14" high. *Courtesy of Majolica Auctions by Michael G. Strawser* $900-1,800

Although unmarked, some have attributed this monkey serving dish to Holdcroft because of the green underside. *Courtesy of Leprechaun Antiques* $1,200-1,400

The head of a stag against a tree trunk serves as a spill vase for Holdcroft. 9.25" high. *Britannia, Grays Antique Market, London* $1,500-2,100

Chapter Four

English Firms:
Limited Productions of Figures

Thomas Forester

In the six years after opening his firm Thomas Forester accomplished more than most pottery manufacturers. According to Jewitt (who spells the name Forrester), after opening his small firm on High Street in 1877, Forester acquired additional property on Church Street. He razed these buildings to build a larger facility in 1879. This new area gave him room to expand, but he soon found that it was not enough. He bought the adjoining china factory which gave him a total of six kilns along with up-to-date equipment. The business continued to grow to become one of the largest in the area. By 1883 the factory employed 400 workers and added "& Sons" to the firm name. The majolica, according to Jewitt, is "remarkably firm and good in body, the colouring well managed, the glaze very satisfactory" (p. 546).

Forester attempted to attract the American market. *The Pottery Gazette* of January 1883 stated of Forester:

> ... his "American" style of business seems to be rushing in where others fear to tread. His productions are being planted in every state in America. . . . Others are keenly competing for the American favours, and it will be interesting to watch the struggle for supremacy.[1]

Forester produced 12,000 floral pots per week in 1895 aided by a machine which produced two pieces per minute. By 1889 Forester no longer advertised his majolica, but apparently did continue production until World War 1.[2]

Although much of Forester's majolica is unmarked, it is identified by green and brown mottling. Perhaps the most noteworthy figure made by Forester, according to Jewitt, is a life-size St. Bernard dog. Modeled by W. W. Gallimore after a champion dog owned by the Bayleys of Shooter's Hill, the figure sits on a 42" pedestal. Forester is perhaps best known for his gurgling fish pitchers. The firm closed in 1959.

Forester figures lack the high quality and attention to detail seen in Minton and Jones figures. Their appeal perhaps stems in part from their whimsical and charming nature. Because a great deal of their majolica was imported into America, their availability probably has a lot to do with their collectibility as well.

Although many times unmarked, Forester figurals have a telltale yellow or green and brown mottled underside that makes attribution possible. These fish are probably by Forester. During the 1880s fish became increasingly popular subjects for figural jugs because of the strong Japanese influence in the decorative arts. Although these jugs are 11" high, they were made in several sizes by a number of manufacturers. *Courtesy of Bertrand Cocq* $275-475

This elephant plant holder with his unusual shell-shaped howdah illustrates the Victorian love of the whimsical. Although unmarked, this piece is attributed to Forester. *Britannia, Grays Antique Market, London* $1,100-1,700

Monks were popular subjects for ale jugs. Legend had it that monks who drank, slept well and monks who slept well, did not sin so they went to heaven! This Forester monk jug came in several sizes from 6" to 11" high. $325-450

Wedgwood majolica is marked with an impressed name in all capital letters accompanied by the three letter date code.

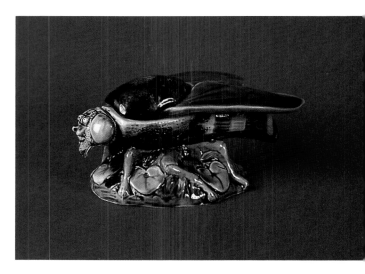

This Wedgwood fly matchbox has a striker inside. Circa 1875. 5" long. *Photography by Jill Graham* $4,000-5,000

Wedgwood

Josiah Wedgwood founded a firm in Burslem in 1759. The firm moved to Etruria in 1769 and established a reputation for fine products. However, by the nineteenth century financial difficulties and poor management reflected in the quality of the products. In 1859 Francis Wedgwood and his eldest son Godfrey attempted to rebuild the firm's reputation. Because of the financial difficulties in the 1850s, Wedgwood was slow in introducing majolica. Having built its reputation on classical designs, there was little motivation to try this new whimsical product. It was not until ten years after Minton had begun production of majolica that Wedgwood commenced manufacturing it. Most of the production centered upon utilitarian wares and very few fanciful pieces were made.

When Wedgwood decided to introduce majolica, he was able to acquire the Minton Patent Ovens invented by Arnoux in large part due to Arnoux's respect for Wedgwood. Carrier-Belleuse and Hugues Protât did freelance work for Wedgwood and in 1860 Émile Lessore left Minton for Wedgwood. Wedgwood introduced new transparent glazes on a white body giving a more brilliant coloring. Since Wedgwood imported clays for their porcelain from as far away as Tennessee, Georgia, and South Carolina,[3] one wonders if some of these clays were used for their majolica as well.

A large part of the majolica figural production reflected the Renaissance Revival style with *putti* figures. Wedgwood did, however, make the wonderful fly match boxes and sea horse centerpieces. In addition, they manufactured some allegorical pieces. Reticulated edges like those on the sea horse centerpiece indicate Wedgwood.

Wedgwood pieces often have reticulated edges like this centerpiece with sea horses. Circa 1871. 8.5" high. *Britannia, Grays Antique Market, London* $1,600-2,100

Another Wedgwood piece with reticulated edges. Wedgwood manufactured only a limited number of human figural pieces and most of these were *putti*. This centerpiece dates from 1867 and is 13" high. $2,000-2,400

This Wedgwood match holder depicting the faces of tragedy and comedy is hard to find. 3.5" high. *Photography by Jill Graham* $600-950

Royal Worcester

The Worcester Porcelain Company was founded in 1751 by Dr. John Wall, Richard Holdship, the Rev. Benjamin Blayney, and Samuel Bradley. The company established a reputation based on their porcelains. Jewitt describes the "fine taste" of the Worcester firm in this manner:

> The mission of the manufacturer is to *create* a pure taste, not to perpetuate and pander to a vicious and barbarous one. ... The Worcester people seem understand this thoroughly, and nothing, even of the most simple design or common use, which is not pure in taste and elegant issues from their works (p. 147-150).

There is some debate as to whether the Worcester firm made very little majolica or whether they simply left much of it unmarked. Marked Worcester majolica is rare, and most of the human figures seem to include *putti*. However, they did manufacture some animal figures like the recumbent camel, a vertical fish rising out of ocean waves, and a heron walking stick stand not unlike the Minton stork.

Witness the great detailing on this recumbent camel with a howdah by Royal Worcester. *Courtesy of Jerry S. Hayes, Oklahoma City, Oklahoma* $3,500-4,500

Worcester used a majolica glaze on a lightweight earthenware body. The figures, often made in porcelain as well, seem rather quietly elegant. The Worcester mark is a crown with a "C" surrounded by four Ws within a circle underneath a crown. In addition there is a two-digit number or a series of dots indicating the year.

Royal Worcester was not an exception when it came to the popularity of monkey designs. This monkey clinging to the side of the vase is unglazed, making a nice contrast both in color and texture to the glazed vase. *Courtesy of Leprechaun Antiques* $800-1,200

Ancient Chinese Buddhists believed that lions could ward off evil spirits. This haughty Royal Worcester lion seems to be ready to take his role seriously! 7.75" high. $4,000-5,500

T. C. Brown-Westhead, Moore & Co.

In 1794 the Cauldon Place firm opened in Hanley. Six years later Job Ridgway built a new plant there and in 1814 took his sons John and William into partnership. William eventually opened his own firm, leaving John with the Cauldon Place site. In 1855 the T. C. Brown-Westhead, Moore, & Co. operated the firm. Mr. Ridgway continued his connection for three years until his death. When W. Moore died in 1866, his brother James entered the business and became a partner in 1875. Upon James' death, his nephew F. T. Moore managed the firm. He expanded the operation. According to Jewitt the "goods [produced were] of a costly character and of great artistic skill and beauty" (p. 493).

Contemporary sources mention a Mr. Bates as partner from 1854 until his retirement in 1861. According to these sources the firm name was then called Bates, Brown-Westhead, Moore, & Co., though Jewitt does not mention Bates at all.

Brown-Westhead, Moore, & Co. attempted to sell to the American market. At the Philadelphia Centennial Exhibition in 1876 they exhibited their majolica and the *General Report of the Judges* commented that it was "well potted" and "good in design and color." The firm manufactured life size tigers, swans, cats, dogs, and other animals which they exhibited at the Paris Exhibition of 1878. The *Crockery & Glass Journal* of that year remarked that the firm's display included "some magnificent specimens of majolica which required considerable space."[4]

Marks for the firm include the name in all block letters in black or the impressed or black initials. Not all of their majolica is marked.

T. C. Brown-Westhead, Moore & Co. made this unusual statuette. Circa 1870. The nineteenth-century consumer was fascinated by tales from travelers. Exotic foreigners as subjects for pottery became increasingly popular. *Photography by Jill Graham* $4,000-5,000

T.C. BROWN-WESTHEAD
MOORE & CO.

Edward Steele

In the beginning of the nineteenth century Thomas Ford opened a pottery firm on Cannon Street in Hanley. Edward Steele acquired the firm in 1875 and operated it until 1900. According to Jewitt the firm produced "earthenware of the more ordinary qualities, stoneware of good useful character, majolica, and Parian" (p.500).

In 1881 the census indicated that the forty-three-year-old Steele employed sixty people. Much of their majolica was unmarked except for a British registry mark. Known for their mouth-pouring pitchers, each shaped like a frog resting upon a lily pad and made in graduated sizes, Steele also made a Falstaff toby jug in majolica.[5]

Edward Steele made only a very few figurals with perhaps the best known being this frog on a lily pad. These were made in several sizes ranging from 3" to 11" high. Dating from 1880, the largest of these frogs is sometimes difficult to find. *Courtesy of Jerry S. Hayes, Oklahoma City, Oklahoma* $1,300-1,700 large size

Shakespeare's Falstaff appeared an appropriate character for a toby jug, yet this Edward Steele example is one of the few English tobies to be manufactured in majolica. Circa 1880s. 10.5" high. *Photography by Jill Graham* $650-900

J & T Bevington

Very little information is available about this firm except that it primarily made parian statuettes and some majolica. James and Thomas Bevington opened a works on Marsh Street in Hanley in 1865 and two years later moved to the Burton Palace Works on New Street, also in Hanley. They ceased manufacturing majolica around 1870,[6] though the firm apparently continued production of earthenware and china under the name Hanley Porcelain Company until 1891.[7] The mark consists of the impressed initials "J. & T. B."

Not a great deal is known about the J. T. Bevington Company, but it made this charming hair-tidy as a Chihuahua playing with a ball of yarn. 6.25" high.
Britannia, Grays Antique Market, London
$800-1,200

William Brownfield & Co.

W. Brownfield & Son erected the Cobridge Works in 1808. It closed in 1819, reopened under James Clews, and closed again ten years later. Robinson, Wood, & Brownfield opened the firm for a third time in 1836, but Robinson died a short time later. When Brown retired in 1850, Brownfield retained control and took his oldest son, William Etches Brownfield, as partner. The name became W. Brownfield & Sons. Around 1871 the firm began the production of majolica which they exhibited at the London Exhibition that year. Jewitt states: "In this material the firm manufactures somewhat largely all the usual ornamental and useful articles known to the trade" (p. 475).

Brownfield figures include the "Isle of Man" teapots which are shaped as a coil of rope upon which sits a three-legged sailor. Some of these teapots have an advertisement reading "W. Broughton, China Room, 50 Duke Street, Douglas." Broughton, a china merchant, commissioned Brownfield's three-legged man teapots to advertise his shop.[8]

Although much Brownfield majolica is unmarked, impressed or printed initials sometimes appear within a Staffordshire knot. Occasionally the British registry mark is on the underside. The firm closed in 1900.

Exotic birds appealed to the nineteenth-century consumer and this wonderful Brownfield cockatoo must have been no exception. Circa 1875. 13.25" high. *Photography by Jill Graham* $2,000-3,000

This miscellaneous grouping of English majolica includes two Isle of Man teapots, probably made by Brownfield, circa 1870. (Holdcroft made a similar tobacco jar.) To the right of the those teapots is a Minton Japanese dwarf teapot, circa 1865, and a Holdcroft Chinaman on a coconut, circa 1875. *Courtesy of William Doyle Galleries Auctioneers & Appraisers* $800-1,000 Isle of Man; $1,500-2,000 Minton; $1,200-1,500 Holdcroft

Chapter Five

French Firms: Major Manufacturers

Sarreguemines:
"The Wedgwood of France"

In 1790 three tobacco merchants from Strasbourg, Nicolas and Augustin Jacoby and Joseph Fabry, established a pottery firm in an old oil mill on the left bank of the Sarre River where it joins the Blies River in Sarreguemines, France. The territory was in the present day Lorraine province in northeastern France, just across the border from Germany. Sarreguemines is pronounced SAR-RUH-GER-MEAN.

The area seemed ideal for manufacturing pottery, with the river to provide treatment for the rich clay in the area as well as transportation for the products, and the Vosges Forest to provide wood to fire the large beehive kilns.

In this town of 2,500 inhabitants the small firm had a slow beginning. Twenty workers were on salary at the factory during this time. In 1799, nearly ten years after it had opened, Fabry decided to summon Paul Utzschneider, an old friend from Strasbourg, to help contribute much needed money to rebuild old equipment. Utzschneider, born in Bavaria in 1771 and trained as a chemist, had studied ceramics in England and in fact had worked for Wedgwood. He had become known for his metallic glazes.[1]

One year after his arrival in Sarreguemines, Utzschneider took control of the factory. The new director bought two new windmills, enlarged the work force to eighty, and operated four kilns. By 1812 the factory employed 160 workers and maintained seven kilns. Utzschneider had doubled his work force and nearly doubled the number of kilns in the twelve years he had directed the factory.[2]

At this time Sarreguemines became quite well-known for its diversified production and for the quality of the wares. In 1819 the factory began decorating its wares with a metallic luster. The tin-glazed earthenware pieces were called "faïence fine." These "opaque porcelain" wares helped establish the reputation of the Sarreguemines factory.

With the Classical Revival in full swing in England, potters there were producing the low relief wares with classical images. Most of the pieces of this period were classical in spirit, but definitely nineteenth century in shape with weight well toward the base on vases and pitchers. The real classical pieces had higher shoulders and a narrower base.

Intrigued by the products of England, Utzschneider sought to emulate them. He created fine stoneware like the jasperware of Wedgwood. Having worked for Wedgwood and offering a line similar to jasperware, Utzschneider became known as "the Wedgwood of France."

The Wedgwood jasperware, a line of blue, green, or black fine stoneware with white bas-relief figures overlaid on the body, was inspired by the Portland vase, a first century A.D. Greco-Roman vase now in the British Museum. Sarreguemines produced a similar line of fine stoneware "in the English manner." The Sarreguemines ware was available with a stoneware-colored ground, rather than the Wedgwood colors.

By the 1830s the "terre d'Egypte" was added to production. Also around this time, Sarreguemines began production of decorations imprinted on bronze plaques which became quite successful. Utzschneider, who had been named a Knight of the Legion of Honor in 1819, continued to refine the techniques, clays, and decorating of the Sarreguemines production. He constantly sought to improve the quality of the wares. The factory was honored by several prizes and medals from national and regional expositions. By this time the factory employed over 300 workers.

Paul Utzschneider retired at the age of sixty-five on July 1, 1836, and ceded direction of the firm to his son-in-law, Baron Alexander de Geiger. Utzschneider moved to Neunkirch-les-Sarreguemines and died there eight years later.

Like his father-in-law, Alexander de Geiger was born in Bavaria. While a student in Augsbourg, he was a classmate of Napoleon Bonaparte. De Geiger received his legal degree in 1830, but married Pauline Utzschneider in 1835 and one year later took control of the firm in Sarreguemines. De Geiger entered politics and became mayor and later Senator of the Empire. Eventually he became Consul General. His influence enabled the town of

Sarreguemines to grow as a transportation center with navigable canals and a developed railway system, improvements which favored the factory.[3]

Under the direction of Alexander de Geiger, the factory undertook expansion. New machines run by steam and turbines enabled a greater diversification. New factories were created along with new products. One such product was a phosphoric porcelain made with kaolin and animal bones, somewhat like the English porcelain. Other expansion plans included association with the families of Villeroy and Boch and with Mettlach.

As the century progressed, the enthusiasm for the stylized figures and controlled discipline of the classical revival waned and interest in naturalism began. Random patterns of plants appeared on much of the pottery of the period because the Paris Exhibition of 1844 had displayed this style. Genre jugs became popular. Most of these jugs had a rounded body with high shoulders.

Hunting and drinking scenes perhaps appealed to the landed gentry who constituted a sizeable segment of the consuming population. Game dishes and tureens depicting the heads of animals appeared on the market. The interest in naturalism continued into the last quarter of the century.

Pauline de Geiger had given birth to a son, Paul, in 1837. By 1864 he became technical director of the factory. During the 1860s Sarreguemines had 2,000 workers, four kilns, and more than 4 million annual gross including a range of products without precedent. In twenty years the factory had increased its work force by 1700. A boat named after Pauline now carried materials between the five production plants along the Sarre River.

Favoring a new printed faïence, Paul de Geiger gradually ceased production of lustered and other "luxury" wares. In addition, he developed a line of industrial wares. In 1865 Sarreguemines returned to production of stoneware in the classical revival mode. Pieces reflecting the Middle Ages, the Renaissance, and even Rococo styles became the trend.[4]

The classical scenes on old jugs began changing to drinking scenes on the English pottery. In addition, the figures of Bacchus and Silenus lent themselves particularly well to jugs made for pubs and their French counterparts. Minton produced a "Silenus Jug" and Sarreguemines copied it.

Yet another creation for tavern use was the toby jug. Though it had originated in the eighteenth century, it gained popularity as the nineteenth century progressed. In addition to the portly "ordinary Toby," other jugs appeared. Sometimes these jugs depicted only the head and shoulders and came to be called character jugs.

The end of the Second Empire came in 1870 with the developing Franco-Prussian War. Alexander de Geiger retired in 1871 and moved to Paris where he died eight years later. Paul de Geiger now had complete control of the company.

In 1874, the Treaty of Frankfurt ceded Lorraine to Germany. To enable his workers to retain their French citizenship, de Geiger opened a factory in Digoin in Saone-et-Loire in 1877 (not to be confused with Dijon in the Burgundy region). Digoin at this time became the center for the production of industrial wares. In 1881 de Geiger opened a warehouse in Vitry-le-François in the Marne region.

De Geiger's daughter married Hippolyte Boulanger, the director of Choisy-le-Roi, and this connection allowed many of Sarreguemines workers who did not wish to become German to move to Choisy. With Sarreguemines under German control and unfashionable for the French market, Choisy began to receive high honors at international exhibitions.

During this period the average age for incoming workers was fourteen years and they generally retired at about seventy years. The work day ranged from 10-12 hours. Many foreign workers were included in the staff, particularly Flemish and English. By the turn of the century, Polish workers accounted for a portion of the work force.

Sarreguemines provided dormitories for staff members and in 1878 built a beautiful casino for the employees. The casino housed a library with books and newspapers in French and German, a gymnasium, a concert hall, and of course, game areas. In summers outdoor events created diversions for the employees.[5]

About 1868 Sarreguemines introduced a new product: majolica. Made from the old stoneware molds, these pieces exhibited the high quality of workmanship that had become synonymous with the name Sarreguemines. At the Paris Exhibition in 1855 Minton's introduction of majolica in France had created a lot of excitement which did not escape the attention of pottery factories on the continent. To produce majolica de Geiger ordered Arnoux kilns from Minton. He eventually installed them in Digoin after opening the factory there.

Sarreguemines majolica is some of the finest ever made. It has a wonderful definition and remarkable coloring with well-defined relief. The attention to detail and excellent quality of their wares surpassed that of other manufacturers, with the exception of Minton. Sarreguemines used a cobalt blue just as Minton did. This blue, like that of the well-known Sèvres porcelain, along with a complementary ochre, became trademark colors of Sarreguemines.

The Pottery & Glass Trades' Review of 1877 noted:

> Mazarine blue is a difficult colour to govern, but this firm has reproduced it on earthenware and majolica in an almost faultless manner.[6]

The Sarreguemines factory made spectacular majolica tile panels, decidedly French. One such panel hangs in the Sarreguemines Museum today. This particular panel depicts attendees at the French races, but was made while Lorraine was part of Germany. The workers at the factory seemed intent upon maintaining their French spirit. Other Sarreguemines majolica items included dessert sets, tobacco jars which averaged 6" to 7" in height, vases, fruit services, articles of "fantasy," pedestals, and of course, character jugs.

Around the turn of the century Sarreguemines employed ten to twelve sales representatives who met annually in Lyon to discuss sales in their respective areas. These representatives made suggestions concerning production of pieces and choice of colors.

By 1907 Sarreguemines employed 3,250 workers and was one of the largest pottery manufacturers in the world. After 1920 Sarreguemines' mark with "D & V" overwritten indicated all three locations.

Just before World War I, Max von Jaunez, a cousin of Paul de Geiger, controlled the factory. Not much is known about Sarreguemines history during the war, but apparently the director of Mettlach, Roger von Boch-Galhau, became the administrator of Sarreguemines. After the war Lorraine again became French and the Cazal family (related to de Geiger through Jaunez) took control of the factories which began making ceramics for ships.[7]

Two views of the Sarreguemines Faïencerie. Circa 1892. *Courtesy of the Musée de Sarreguemines*

The Casino of the Faïencerie and the Paul de Geiger Pavilion. Circa 1892. *Courtesy of the Musée de Sarreguemines*

A 1923 photograph of the filter presses at the faïencerie. *Courtesy of the Musée de Sarreguemines*

The enameling studio at the Sarreguemines Faïencerie. Circa 1923. *Courtesy of the Musée de Sarreguemines*

A photo of the artists' studio at the Sarreguemines Faïencerie. Circa 1923. *Courtesy of the Musée de Sarreguemines*

Majolica began to decline in fashion in France, and Sarreguemines discontinued its production sometime around 1930. However, they continued as a leading manufacturer of other types of pottery well into the twentieth century. During World War II, the firm of Villeroy and Boch controlled the Sarreguemines factory.

Gradually all production began to decline and by 1983 the Sarreguemines factories closed. The nearby factory of St. Clément bought the old molds and began reproducing some of the old majolica patterns. These consisted of fruit and dessert sets and table services. Only a very few figurals are being produced. The dominant portion of the figural reproduction consists of previously popular St. Clément and Sarreguemines designs.[8]

These reproductions are marked either St. Clément or Sarreguemines depending upon the original manufacturer. However, they are easily distinguished from the originals because they lack the wonderful subtlety and definition of the originals and are much lighter weight. Today the old factory houses an outlet store where these reproductions are sold.

The old dormitory, factory, casino, and several production buildings, the Utzschneider residence, and one bottle kiln remain. The residence houses the wonderful Sarreguemines Museum dedicated to the preservation of factory artifacts. Currently a new building is being added to the museum where old molds and records will be displayed.

A catalog page from the Sarreguemines Faïencerie listing all three locations. Circa 1925. *Courtesy of the Musée de Sarreguemines*

Sarreguemines figural jugs include such stylized birds as the raven (no. 3567) and the owl (no. 3566). *Courtesy of "Marty"* $300-400 each

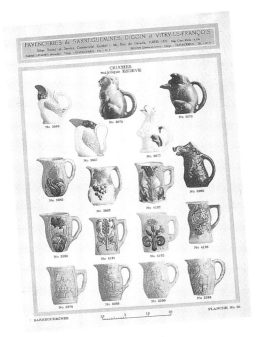

A page from the 1925 catalog of the Sarreguemines Faïencerie showing the "Esdeve" line. *Courtesy of the Musée de Sarreguemines*

The cat (no. 3675) from the "Esdeve" line also came in black and white. $300-400

The Sarreguemines dog (no. 3677).

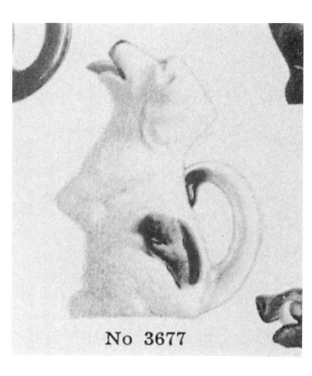

No 3677

A catalog page showing more of the Sarreguemines animal figural pitchers. *Courtesy of the Musée de Sarreguemines*

The ocean birds like the sea gull (no. 3527) and the dog (no. 3677) made charming figurines. Difficult to find. *Courtesy of "Marty"*
$300-500 each

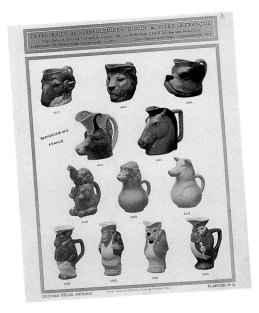

A 1925 catalog page showing animal jugs, five of which are character jugs of the animals. *Courtesy of the Musée de Sarreguemines*

The Sarreguemines lion's head (no. 4020) and the bulldog's head (no. 4024) have wonderful detail in the fur. *Courtesy of "Marty"* $350-450 lion; $550-650 dog

This Sarreguemines stylized monkey jug (no, 3322) was copied by English manufacturers, but it is not difficult to tell them apart. *Courtesy of "Marty"* $350-475

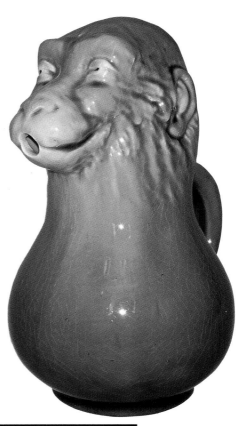

Sarreguemines manufactured these pig jugs (no. 3318) for a period of years. The oldest has only one hole in his snout; the later versions had two, then three holes. The English copy of this piece has a yellowish exterior and is unmarked. *Courtesy of "Marty"* $300-450

Sarreguemines animal figures included egg cups and game dishes as witnessed by this catalog page. *Courtesy of the Musée de Sarreguemines*

An unusual griffin figure (no. 903), possibly a special order. *Courtesy of Bertrand Cocq* Rare in this design.

A pheasant (no. 4451) game dish shown in the catalog page. *Courtesy of "Marty"* $150-250

This bull paperweight, circa 1875, has the impressed "Majolica" mark which was discontinued after 1890. This piece was still shown in the catalog after the turn of the century, indicating its popularity. *Courtesy of the Musée de Sarreguemines*

Marks

Sarreguemines marked virtually all of their jugs, though rarely a piece did escape unmarked. Majolica pieces have the name impressed in block letters on the base of the piece, occasionally accompanied by the number of the mold and the type of product. Sarreguemines made 6,000 different types of products, so their range was extensive. Character jugs and majolica figures carry the #227 for majolica.

Between 1898 and 1905 Sarreguemines numbered character jugs with the month and year of production. The letter on the bottom indicates the decorator, not the designer, since decorators were paid by the piece.

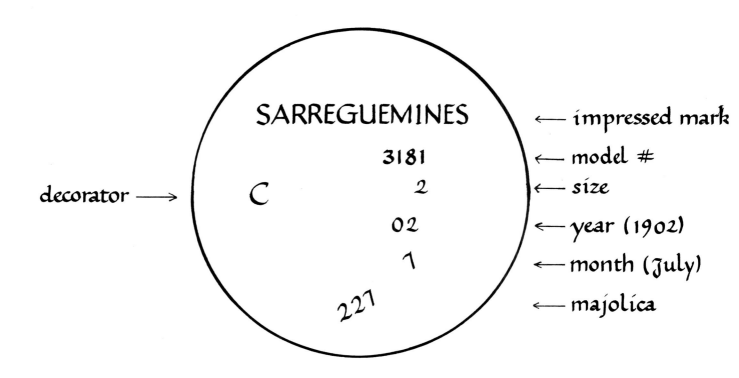

decorator ⟶

SARREGUEMINES ⟵ impressed mark
3181 ⟵ model #
2 ⟵ size
02 ⟵ year (1902)
7 ⟵ month (July)
227 ⟵ majolica

C

A 1925 catalog page still showing the five sizes of the popular no. 3181 model. These jugs date from the turn of the century. *Courtesy of the Musée de Sarreguemines*

After the passage of the McKinley Tariff Act of 1891 which required that all imports be marked with the country of origin, Sarreguemines had to add "France" under the manufacturer's name for pieces it displayed at the Chicago Exposition of 1894. However, it was not until after 1918 that Sarreguemines pieces regularly carried the name of the country. Some French pieces are marked "deposé" indicating that the design was registered for export.

Around 1868 MAJOLICA appeared impressed in capital letters, but was discontinued after 1890. The black Lorraine crest with the words "Made in Germany" in English was used during World War I. The name Sarreguemines in black script with "U & C" overwritten dates from 1850 until 1920. The name with "D & V" overwritten dates from 1920 to 1950.

On more recent pieces a stylized, block "S" appears in brown, with or without the country underneath. This mark dates from 1950 and is still seen on pieces made by St. Clément from the old Sarreguemines molds.

The large "jolly fellow," as the jug (no. 3181) is sometimes called, often carries the "Made in Germany" Lorraine crest indicating that the jug was manufactured while Sarreguemines was under German control. $225-375

Since the jugs were hand decorated, each has a distinctive appearance. $150-225

The three smaller sizes of the no. 3181 are sometimes harder to find than the larger ones. $175-300

Solid colored versions appeared in several different models, including the no. 3181. $100-125

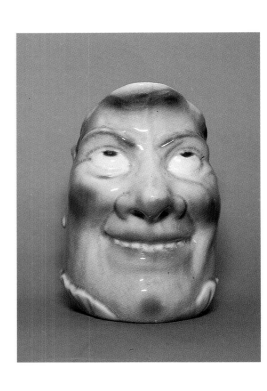

This jug (no. 3258) is listed in the museum registry simply as "upward eyes." $275-375

The John Bull character jug (no. 3257) appeared in two sizes, both with and without the name on the back. $225-325

Though one of the oldest character jugs, the Puck jug (no. 652 and 653) is one of the most common simply because it was manufactured for many years making more of them available for collectors. The jug still appeared in the catalog as late as 1925. Ones with the pewter lid, however, are more difficult to find. Lids like this one were probably intended to keep flies out of the ale. $175-225; $250 with lid

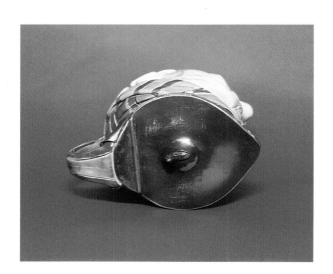

The "Boozer" (no. 3323) as the jug was called, appeared in two sizes. This jug is difficult to find. $375-500

Sarreguemines clowns are rare and highly collectible. Only two different models appeared on the market. This model (no. 4638) appears happy. *Courtesy of "Marty"* $500-650

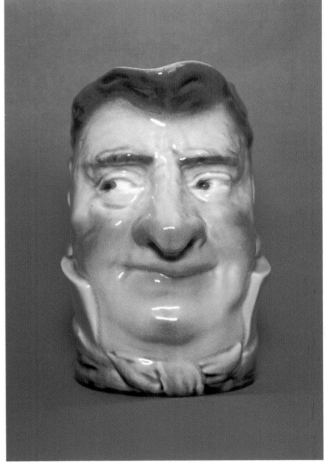

The sad clown (no. 4639) is one of the latest character jugs made by Sarreguemines, but it was also made in limited quantities not long before the firm discontinued production of majolica. $500-650

Simply listed as "high collar" (no. 3297) in the museum registry, this jug has acquired a variety of nicknames. $250-350

Though this fellow appears to have a toothache and has acquired that nickname, it is listed as "the headband" (no. 3321). This hard to find jug came in two sizes. $450-600

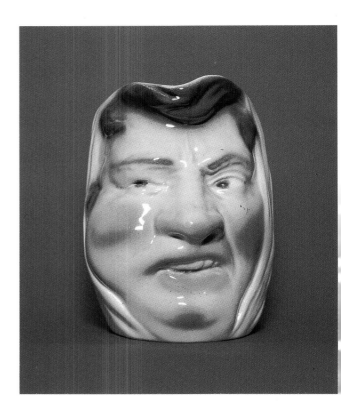

Listed as "Suspicious eyes" (no. 3320), this jug is often called "the Admiral." The black mark with the name of the country dates this piece to 1920 or later. $225-325

This jug, known as "the English" (no. 3210), came in only one size both with and without the phrase "V'la les English." It also came in solid green. One of the most common jugs. $225-325

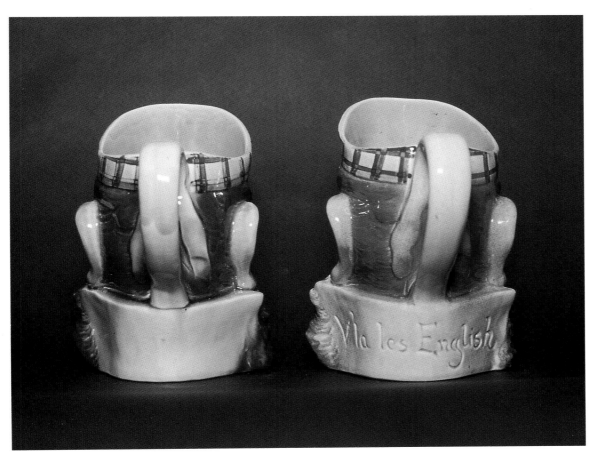

A catalog page showing teapots and character jugs made by Sarreguemines. *Courtesy of the Musée de Sarreguemines*

This Uncle Sam jug (no. 4316) obviously appealed to a particular market! *Courtesy of "Marty" Rare*

Listed as a "French Soldier" (no. 4305), this jug has the impressed mark with the name of the country below it. *Courtesy of the Musée de Sarreguemines*

The "Russian Head" (no. 3300) appears to be a young prince and has acquired that nickname. *Courtesy of "Marty"* $500-675

This very rare character jug, found in India, has a removable lid and matte finish face. Though unmarked it has been verified as Sarreguemines. *Courtesy of "Marty"* $400-500

The lady with a crown (no. 3331) represents a Norwegian lady, presumably royalty. *Courtesy of Bertrand Cocq* $400-550

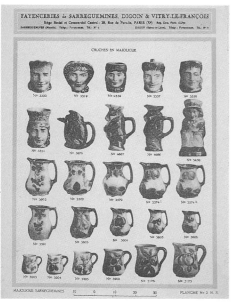

A catalog page showing female character jugs. *Courtesy of the Musée de Sarreguemines*

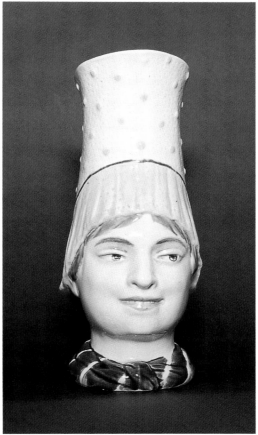

Female versions of the character jugs are usually more valuable, since fewer were manufactured. The one with the bonnet is listed as a "Danish woman" (no.3319) while the tall hat represents one of the oldest female jug designs. It is 9.5" high and listed as a "Normandy jug" (no.1752). Circa 1880s. The woman with blonde hair (no. 3358) is listed as just that in the registry. $400-600 each

A catalog page showing a character jug along with tobies and jardinieres. *Courtesy of the Musée de Sarreguemines*

Called the "judge" (no. 4502) this jug came in two sizes; the smaller stands 6.5" high and the larger 7.5" high. The larger is more difficult to find. *Courtesy of "Marty"* $225-350

A catalog page indicates that Sarreguemines manufactured three blackamoor character jugs, but these are extremely rare. *Courtesy of the Musée de Sarreguemines*

This jolly face seems a variation of the no. 3181, but is simply listed as a "jug" in the registry. A goatee was added and a hat (no. 3611). $250-350

The Napoleon jug (no. 4610) is nicely modeled with good coloring. Because it was one of the latest jugs and because it is cross-collected, this jug is difficult to find. The "P.V." mark probably indicates an importer. $500-750

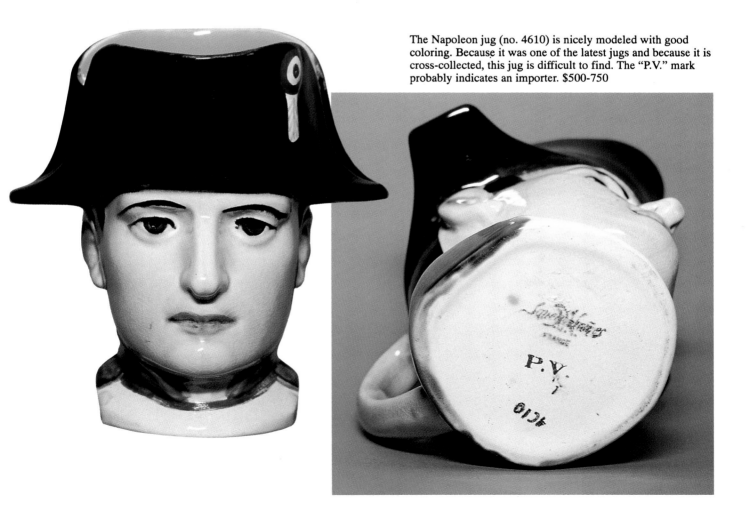

This very rare toby (no. 1197) has the impressed mark along with "majolica." Circa 1880. Rare

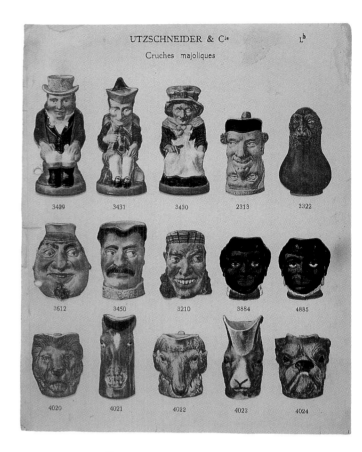

A 1905 catalog page showing the few toby jugs made by Sarreguemines. *Courtesy of the Musée de Sarreguemines*

This toby figure of John Bull (no. 3429) is sometimes referred to as the "Bourgeois Capitalist." However, in all probability, the jug was made for the English market, so it stands to reason that it represents the patriotic symbol of England. 13" high. $695-895

Listed only as "two superimposed heads" (no. 2313), this jug has a phrase in French around the bottom. A solid green version of this jug exists. (Caution-if the phrase is in English, it is a reproduction.) *Courtesy of the Musée de Sarreguemines* $375-450

Punch and Judy became popular characters in Victorian England, so these tobies were obviously made for the English market. The bases on these jugs are turquoise, unlike other Sarreguemines jugs. Both are around 13" high. $750-950 Punch (no. 3431); $450-525 Judy (no. 3430)

Staffordshire Punch and Judy toby jugs have an entirely different appearance. Their white faces have features painted in fine lines, their clothes have more intense colors like oranges or greens, and their crowns are removable. Moreover, they are not as tall as the Sarreguemines ones. NP

Two hard to find Sarreguemines jugs. The one in blue is presumably General Ferdinand Foch who commanded the Allied troops in World War I. The one in the black hat is Francis Joseph, emperor of Austria (1848-1916) and king of Hungary (1867-1916). *Courtesy of Jacques Salzard* $450-650 each

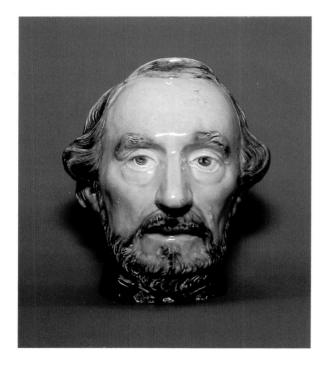

Bartolomé Mitre (no. 3726) was the president of Argentina from 1862 to 1868. Under his presidency the country advanced rapidly. This jug was perhaps commissioned from Sarreguemines to commemorate the 100th year of Mitré's birth in 1821. These jugs are rare since they only appeared in Argentina. $500-700

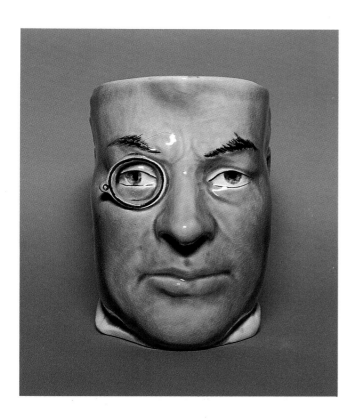

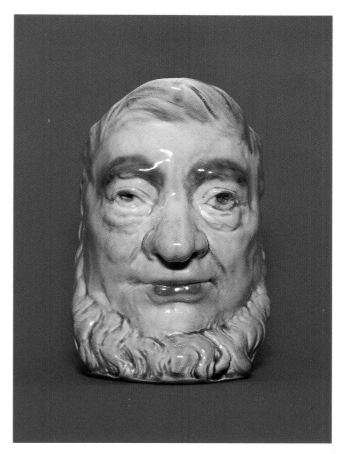

Listed in the Sarreguemines registry only as "Chamberlain" (no. 3466), this 5.5" jug presumably represents Joseph Chamberlain who was a member of Gladstone's cabinet from 1880-1885. He became the Colonial Secretary of England from 1895 to 1903. Chamberlain favored expansion in Africa. *Courtesy of "Marty"* $450-600

The Paul Kruger Sarreguemines jug (no. 3185) appeared in three sizes and all are hard to find. Kruger headed the Boer republic of the Transvaal in South Africa during the war with Great Britain. He came to France in 1900 to raise money for his war efforts. After the war Kruger became the president of the Transvaal in 1883 after it regained its independence. This was probably a commissioned piece. $395-525

Dranem was a turn of the century comedian immortalized by Sarreguemines and Nimy. Actors and comedians became trendy subjects during the late nineteenth century. *Courtesy of Bertrand Cocq* $450-550

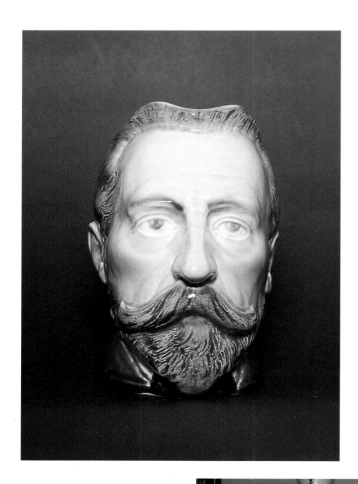

Chairman Michelsen was the prime minister of Norway. This very rare piece (no. 3733) was probably commissioned by Norway since Sarreguemines exported to that country. 6" high. $400-600

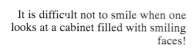

It is difficult not to smile when one looks at a cabinet filled with smiling faces!

The Legends of Beer

Legends about beer and ale abound. In most of these legends the secret of beer-making is always a gift of a goddess, never a god. Ino, a mythological woman, tempted the baby Bacchus to love fermented grape juice, and he became the patron saint of drinkers. In ancient Sumeria women ran taverns, protected by Siduri, patron saint of wisdom and goddess of the brewery.

As far back as 2300 B.C. an Egyptian Pharaoh charter stated that God loved the world so much that He gave women the ability to make beer. Beer allowed God's children to commune with Him through tribal celebrations.

Hieroglyphics from around 1350 B.C. during the rule of Ramses II refer to temperance in drinking beer because of the consequences of drunkenness. The ancient hieroglyphic for food was a picture of a loaf of bread and a pitcher of beer. Egyptian dead were buried with bread and beer for their journey to the next life. The rich were buried with entire breweries!

Ancient Egyptians believed that the Goddess Hathor, Queen of Drunkenness, invented beer accidentally when she was trying to destroy mankind. Nile dwellers used beer extensively, including when anointing newborns and paying laborers a day's salary.

Pottery is the oldest art form and vessels for beer are among some of the oldest containers found. Anglo-Saxon cups and ancient pitchers made only for beer have been unearthed. Since fermentation enhanced the nutritional values in grain and fermented liquids are non-perishable, it is easy to understand the value of beer in ancient cultures.

Eighteenth- and Nineteenth-Century Drinking Habits

The first half of the eighteenth century in England is often referred to as the cheap gin period. While upper classes drank ale or wine, and politicians drank port and champagne or claret, the poor drank quantities of gin. Gin houses offered warmth and hospitality from the streets.

Hogarth's depiction of the horrors of "Gin's Lane" compared to the prosperous "Beer Street" began to turn public opinion away from gin. The "Act of 1751" which taxed spirits helped reduce their consumption.

A eighteenth-century canon of St. Paul's Cathedral states, "The immense importance of a pint of ale to a common person should never be overlooked."[9] This belief that beer relieved the stress of everyday life for the common man was widespread. In the nineteenth century Charles Dickens captures the appeal of the tavern as a respite from the inhospitable streets in his novel *Barnaby Rudge*:

> The ruddy gleam of the fire . . . seemed
> to bring with it, as part of itself, a pleasant
> hum of voices, and a fragrant odour of
> steaming grog and rare tobacco, all steeped
> as it were in cheerful glow . . . from the
> distant kitchen a gentle sound of frying,
> with a musical clatter of plates and dishes,
> and a savoury smell. ... He tried to look
> stoically at the tavern, but his features
> would relax into a look of fondness.[10]

The Beer Act of 1830 gave beer houses relief from buying a justice license, so public houses (pubs) increased. Beer or ale jugs, some with lids for keeping out flies, became popular. Sometimes these jugs remained on a shelf or hanging behind the pub's bar for a patron who stopped regularly to socialize with friends. At other times beer was "fetched" from the pub or local inn and taken home to drink.

In the Victorian homes beer dispensers allowed servants to receive some of their salary in drink. Local pubs owned by employers allowed trade people to pick up their salary there or they could take their wages in drink.[11]

Brewers were respected, often titled, figures. Of the 48,000 licensed pubs in 1816, 14,200 were owned by brewers. The daughters of brewers were respectable enough to marry landed gentry.[12]

Pubs and inns acted as a local post office where travelers could get mail and read the paper. Most pubs had a working class or lower class clientele and served only beer or ale, not strong liquor. Perhaps one reason for the popularity of beer was the danger in drinking impure water. Tea and liquor were safer, but tea was expensive because of import duties. Since corn, wheat, and barley were available, alcohol was cheap.

Flasks made to represent contemporary political figures became fashionable around the 1830s. The Victorian concept of ornament suggesting purpose caused manufacturers to create specially designed jugs for ale. Minton's "hop jug" is a wonderful example. Later in the century wonderful majolica toby jugs and character jugs appeared on the scene. Since monasteries often produced beer as a means of support, monks became popular figures for ale jugs because of their reputed fondness for drink. A German monk once said: "He who drinks beer sleeps well. He who sleeps well cannot sin. He who does not sin goes to Heaven. Amen."[13]

By the early twentieth century many breweries and pubs advertised on character jugs, a testament to their popularity. English distributors ordered jugs from local companies and from companies in France and then placed their logos on the jugs. Some collectors specialize in collecting advertising jugs.

Beer is one of the oldest of beverages, but the figure of the barmaid became most popular in nineteenth century majolica. 9.25" high. *Courtesy of Majolica Auctions by Michael G. Strawser* $100-150

The History of Toby Jugs

The origin of toby jugs is unknown, though speculation abounds. Pottery jugs in the shape of humans were made thousands of years before Christ, but it was not until the eighteenth century that the term "toby jug" appeared. Perhaps the name refers to the character in Shakespeare's comedy *Twelfth Night*, Sir Toby Belch, a foolish man fond of drink. Other possibilities include Harry Elwes, from Yorkshire, who reportedly consumed 2,000 gallons of beer from a brown jug. Mr. Elwes' nickname was "Toby Fillpot."

A challenger to the Elwes' theory was the story of a man named Paul Parnel. In 1810 in England the *Gentleman's Magazine* stated that Mr. Parnel drank a million pints of strong ale in a sixty-year period! Supposedly he drank this ale "out of one silver pint cup upwards of 9,000 pounds sterling-worth of Yorkshire Stingo. . . . The calculation is taken at two pence per cupful."

The most commonly accepted origin of the toby jug comes from a mezzotint produced by Robert Deighton in 1761. The picture of a very portly, seated gentleman holding a foaming brown jug of ale in one hand and a pipe in the other illustrated a song by the Reverend Francis Faulkes entitled, "The Brown Jug," which was published in a book of poems.

The song, a humorous adaptation of a Latin poem, has a reference to "Toby Fillpot, a thirsty old soul" in the third line. The dress of the gentleman in the mezzotint is appropriate for the period and seems an obvious model for the early English tobies.

It is possible that when Rev. Faulkes penned the line, the name "Toby" may have been a common reference to heavy drinkers at the time. When the poem and picture were further popularized as a comic opera at Covent Garden in 1783, it was an immediate success, so much so that members of Parliament are known to have quoted it![14]

In northern Europe faïence jugs representing human figures appeared in the sixteenth century. The origin of these figures is unknown, but legend has it that Jacqueline, Duchess of Hainaut in Belgium, modeled pots in the shape of people while imprisoned in a dungeon. She would throw them through her window where villagers would gather them. Faïence jugs in the shape of entire, usually seated, figures became known as *Jacquelines* if female, and *Jacquelins* if male.[15]

Many potters have made claims to the first toby jug. Perhaps it was John Voyez, the Frenchman working for Ralph Wood, who modeled the portly man into history. Voyez had worked for Josiah Wedgwood, but was fired for drunkenness. Evidence indicates that he at least had some influence in the shaping of the first Wood tobies. These eighteenth-century English creamware and pearlware tobies are highly collectible today.

The crowns of the original English tobies were removable, intended for use as a cup. Gradually, however, this custom disappeared. Character jugs, which developed later, were very rarely made with crowns. Whatever the origin of these wonderful jugs, they became successful pottery ventures and the fashion spread to the continent.

With the development of majolica in the last half of the nineteenth century, it was inevitable that toby jugs be made in this medium. In France, the Sarreguemines factory began developing its production of majolica around 1870. Tobies and character jugs had maintained their popularity in England, so they seemed a good subject for this new venture. In addition to Sarreguemines, other French and German factories made majolica tobies.

Sarreguemines produced a line of character jugs and animal jugs, but only a few full-figured toby jugs. Most of the character jugs depicted stereotypes like the Englishman, the Danish woman, and the Norwegian. Some, however, were special orders and depicted particular individuals, oftentimes political figures. The toby jugs included the English characters of John Bull, or Punch, and Judy, indicating perhaps these were all made for the English market.

John Bull wrote the earliest version of the English national anthem. In 1712 John Arbuthnot created the character as a symbol for England. It appeared on creamware jugs and Pratt type jugs in the late eighteenth century. *Punch* magazine popularized the character of John Bull in the nineteenth century. In 1900 William Kent manufactured a John Bull toby jug which is remarkably similar to the one by Sarreguemines. The English figure holds in one hand a sheet of paper, sometimes with the word "account" at the top, and in the other a bag of money.[16] The Sarreguemines toby holds a bag of money in each hand. Sometimes called the "Bourgeois Capitalist" or the "Landlord," all indications are that the figure really represents John Bull.

In the case of the tobies, it appears that perhaps Sarreguemines copied English jugs for the English market. On the other hand, England copied successful jugs by Sarreguemines. Since there were no copyright laws protecting pottery designs, factories openly copied each other. In addition, the potters moved from one factory to another, sometimes taking molds with them. If a product proved commercially successful, it was not long before a similar example appeared on the market manufactured by another factory. These copies were often unmarked in the hopes that they would be mistaken for the original.

"Copies" refer to pieces made during the production period of the original, while "reproduction" refers to recently made duplicates. The price for copies runs slightly less than that of the original because copies are usually unmarked. Reproductions, on the other hand, are much newer and consequently much less valuable.

Sarreguemines made character jugs generally in two or three sizes, although one model (no. 3181) came in five sizes ranging from 5" to 8.25" high. Some models came in only one size. If the jug came in two sizes, the smaller one was around 6" high with the larger one somewhere between 7" and 8" high. Unless otherwise noted the pieces pictured fall into this range. Some jugs also appeared in solid colors, but their value is usually less than the others even though they are often more rare. The female examples cost slightly more than the males, simply because fewer models appeared. Smaller pieces often bring as much as larger ones since not as many have survived.

Sarreguemines figures were numbered consecutively within their category from the date of design. The Puck character jugs with a number of 652 is one of the oldest jug designs. However, this jug is also one of the most common simply because it was manufactured for a longer period of time, meaning more exist today. On the other hand, some of the more recent models are rare because they appeared on the market not long before majolica production ceased, so fewer exist.

Since some examples of Sarreguemines character jugs were made for export to countries such as Australia, Armenia, and Argentina, these examples are rare and hard to find in the United States. When a collector does indeed stumble across one, the price reflects the rarity. Examples of these jugs are included for informational purposes only, as the average collector may not have the opportunity to purchase one.

During the Franco-Prussian War when Sarreguemines became German, workers were allowed three years to become German citizens. Many refused and sought employment elsewhere. Twenty-five percent of the workers at the factory emigrated. Many went to Paris, but others went to Italy, French Canada, Argentina, and Buffalo, New York.

Those who immigrated to Buffalo all were employed at the same factory where they made products similar to Sarreguemines. In addition, many went to Algeria because the government was trying to establish a French presence there and gave land to Frenchmen who would settle it. Others sought passage to Australia.

France also minted money for many foreign countries. These connections with other countries along with a reputation for quality products and former employees spread around the globe helped establish Sarreguemines as a leading pottery manufacturer, not only in France but throughout the civilized world. Orders for jugs arrived from Norway, Spain, Switzerland, Russia, Turkey, Germany, Belgium, and Amsterdam in addition to the countries already mentioned. Many of these countries placed special orders for commemorative pieces.

Toby jugs were not intended for royalty. They were the working man's luxury. How pleasant it must have been to wander into a pub at the end of a long, tiring workday and see the jolly face of one's special jug just waiting to be filled with a favorite brew!

Toby jugs as well as character jugs seem to have a charm that escapes some items from the Victorian era. Perhaps it is because these jugs were intended for socializing and not for personal use like a mug or glass. It is difficult not to smile when one looks at a row of smiling faces. Perhaps therein lies the reason for more and more collectors entering the field each day. The number of collectors has grown steadily in recent years as prices will confirm.

Variations on a Theme

Sarreguemines character jugs, especially no. 3181, sometimes appear with advertising logos. Liquor distributors in England ordered them to promote their product. As testament to their popularity, factories in England and on the continent began producing a similar model.

English copies of the Sarreguemines character jugs appeared around the turn of the twentieth century. The English copies, made during the same period of production as the originals, differed in clay and coloring. They generally weigh more, have a whiter body, and have blue-red cheeks rather than coral-colored, with bluish or grayish skin-tones. In addition, the English character jugs consist of white interiors. In a few cases the interiors of English pieces are turquoise, but it is a dull, bluish color rather than the bright turquoise of Sarreguemines. The English coloring lacks interest and clarity. Deep blue-reds, along with lime greens, oranges, and muddy browns appeared.

In addition to unmarked copies, marked copies appeared. Foley and Fielding in England openly copied the middle size of the no. 3181 pattern which came in five sizes from Sarreguemines. The Fielding and Foley jugs are lighter, thinner potted, and have nice detail with nice coloring.

The Foley jugs have softer more subtle coloring. They are thinly potted and have a light turquoise lining around the interior of the rim much like the Fielding ones. The Foley Faience Company, called the Wileman & Company, Foley Potteries and Foley China Works was begun in 1892 by James and Charles Wileman. The firm closed in 1925. The brown mark consists of an interlaced "C" and "W" with a small crown above. "The Foley Faience" appears over the initials and "England" below. These marks often are missing, but both Foley and Fielding jugs are easy to distinguish from the unmarked jugs.

Simon Fielding established Railway Pottery in 1870 on Sutherland Street in Stoke-on-Trent. Around the turn of the century the firm marketed Sarreguemines look-alikes. The brown mark included a lion standing on a crown with "S.F. & Co." above it. In addition, a raised square with a two-digit number, presumably indicating the pattern, appeared near the base rim. Many times these marks have worn away and only the gently raised square is visible.

Sarreguemines jugs have nice detail, a heavier feel, and better coloring. More accurate flesh tones and an entire interior of turquoise differentiate them from copies. Technically these jugs are true majolica while the Fielding and Foley examples are faïence which consists of a harder clay and thinner glaze. By way of explanation, faïence is a French word, but when English firms used it they omitted the umlaut above the letter "i."

Josef Strnact of Turn-Teplitz, Germany, also manufactured a similar jug. The company began in 1881 as a terra cotta factory and shop for decorating porcelain. It closed in 1932. Strnact pieces are marked with a "J" and "S" within a shield and a four-digit number below.[17] Less coloring but very nice detail, lighter pink cheeks which have a slightly speckled appearance, and tan colored faces separate them from similar jugs.

Perhaps one of the most popular patterns ever made by Sarreguemines, the no. 3181 model, also came in stoneware from Sarreguemines. Other copies included porcelain examples, probably made in Germany.

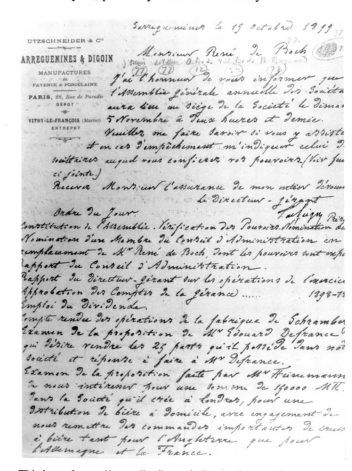

This letter from a liquor distributor in England was written to Sarreguemines in October of 1899 proposing a joint venture. *Courtesy of Villeroy & Boch/Archives*

Several different models of Sarreguemines jugs exhibit advertisements for English liquor companies, presumably following that joint venture. Shown here: two popular sizes of the no. 3181 jolly faced jug with liquor logos. *Courtesy of "Marty"* $200-350

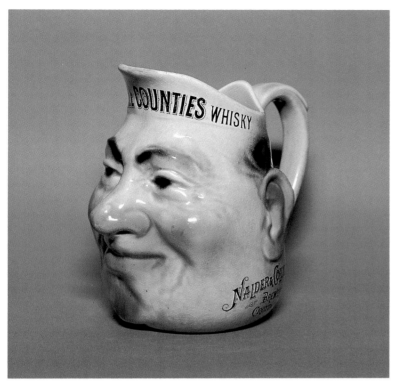

This smaller Sarreguemines no. 3181 was copied by both Fielding and Foley, English factories. *Courtesy of Pam Ferrazzutti Antiques, Toronto* $200-275

The John Bull jug also appeared with advertisements. *Courtesy of "Marty"* $250-350

Even the Sarreguemines pig appeared with advertisements. *Courtesy of Bertrand Cocq* $300-400

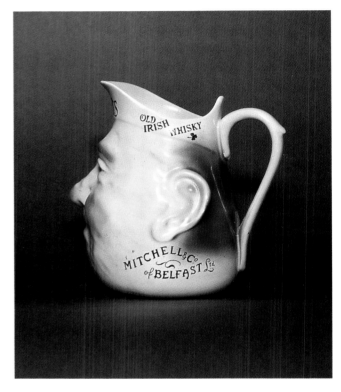

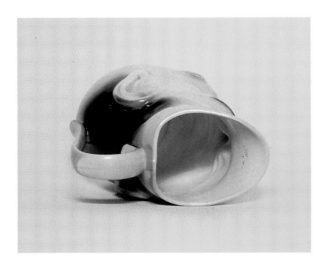

Simon Fielding manufactured a jug like the Sarreguemines model, perhaps indicating the popularity of the joint venture advertising jugs. The Fielding example is lighter weight with only a hint of turquoise in the interior. The mark is often worn away, although it is still visible on this jug. $175-250

Foley is another company that copied the Sarreguemines jug. *Courtesy of "Marty"* $175-250

Many English copies of the popular no. 3181 jugs are unmarked like these copies on either side of a Sarreguemines jug. Compare the whiter bodies and the lack of attention to detail. $100-125 each

Some English copies have a turquoise interior which is much darker than the Sarreguemines interiors of the same color. This English jug has blue undertones compared to the yellow undertones of the French jugs. $125-225

Red is an unusual color for this English copy of the no. 3181 jug. *Courtesy of "Marty"* $75-100

The many variations of the popular Sarreguemines jug include an overall tan jug with little coloring. *Courtesy of M & G Bottero Antiquites, Nice* $100-135

Yet another variation of the no. 3181. The green bow and the blue undertones of the red cheeks indicate that the jug is probably of English origin. $120-160

The jug on the left is a very rare stoneware example made by Sarreguemines. The jug on the right is porcelain, probably German. *Courtesy of "Marty"* $100-250 each

This variation is marked "J" and "S" within a shield, the mark of the Josef Strnact Company in Germany. Whether this jug is a copy of the Sarreguemines or whether Sarreguemines copied this jug is anybody's guess. The 3181 jugs are sometimes called "Joseph": perhaps this jug by Josef Strnact explains the name. Could it have been modeled after the owner of the company? *Courtesy of "Marty"* $125-185

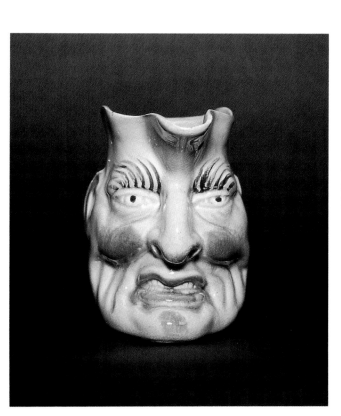

Two different versions of English character jugs. The priest has the skin tones of English pieces as does the Punch character. $150-200 priest; $195-295 Punch

A catalog page showing the Sarreguemines offerings of tobacco jars. *Courtesy of the Musée de Sarreguemines*

The lid of this Sarreguemines tobacco jar is usually missing. According to the catalog page, the lid had a vase with the word "operas" written on it, resting upon the piano top. *Courtesy of Bertrand Cocq* $800-1,500 without lid.

This proud "toreador" is a very rare tobacco jar. *Courtesy of the Musée de Sarreguemines*

This tobacco jar looks like an English gentleman. $225-350

The interest in *Chinoiserie* did not escape Sarreguemines tobacco jars. $185-295

This China girl's lid is missing, but her rarity still makes her interesting to collectors. *Courtesy of "Marty"* $50-75 without lid

The fez hat on the tobacco jar indicates the extent of the interest in *Des Indes* figures. *Courtesy of "Marty"* $225-350

The "child cooper" tobacco jar has turquoise inside the barrel which holds the tobacco. *Courtesy of "Marty"* $400-600

The minstrel holder for pipe lighters (or perhaps spill vase), 12" high, displays advertisements for the Salvation Army (no. 1845). Circa 1880. *Courtesy of "Marty"* $750-900

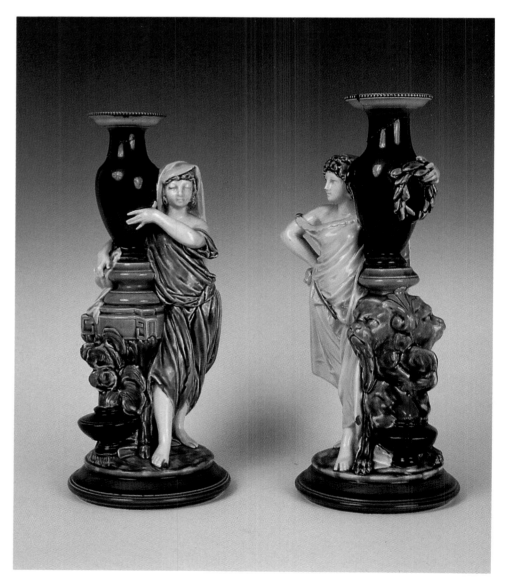

These very elegant candleholders (no. 2241) exhibit the beautiful Sarreguemines cobalt and ochre color combination. *Courtesy of the Musée de Sarreguemines*

Sarreguemines-Type Character Jugs

Throughout history the northern part of France has been in the path of marching armies, from the Vikings to Napoleon to both World Wars. In addition, 90% of France's coal and a large part of its iron come from this area. Because of large deposits of resources needed by armies for fuel, much of the land in the area has suffered repeated destruction over the centuries.

This region also has rich clay as well as forests and streams: important resources needed by pottery manufacturers. Hundreds of majolica producers, cottage industries as well as major manufacturers, located their factories in northern France and in nearby Belgium and Germany. Unfortunately, during World Wars I and II most of the records, catalogs, and designs of these factories were destroyed. Without factory records it is difficult to determine with any accuracy exactly where these factories were located. Such is the case with a particular line of character jugs.

Because of the telltale turquoise lining and numbers on the bottom of each piece, these jugs are frequently sold as Sarreguemines. They were not, however, made at Sarreguemines. In all probability they were made somewhere nearby, either in France or in Germany.

Complete factory records do exist for Sarreguemines productions, but no records include any figures like these jugs. Moreover, when Sarreguemines ceased its majolica production around 1930, their character jugs designs were the 5,000 series. Since all Sarreguemines jugs' designs were numbered consecutively from the date production commenced, it is possible to say with certainty that no jugs were made in either the 7,000 or 8,000 series, and the unidentified jugs carry these series of numbers.

The Sarreguemines-type character jugs are lighter in weight and more thinly potted than actual Sarreguemines pieces. They are also marked with a four digit number beginning with a seven or an eight. The coloring on these jugs includes burgundy, dull blue, purple or olive green: colors never found on Sarreguemines characters. Also the skin tone is not as rich and the eyes are black, not brown, blue, or gray as is the case on most Sarreguemines.

Perhaps as many as twenty different models exist from this manufacturer and many models were made in three, four, or five sizes. The smallest size is 3" while the largest is 8.5" high. The size is indicated by a Roman numeral following the Arabic number. Numeral III indicates the largest size on these jugs whereas the numeral I represents Sarreguemines' largest size. Besides jugs, bottles also exist. In some cases the model for the bottle is the same as a jug, but the mold number is different. Whether these bottles were used for liquor, ink, or something else entirely is anybody's guess.

Collectors have nicknamed this Sarreguemines-type jug "the Scotsman" (no. 7889). The tallest is 8.25" high, with the next two measuring 7" and 6" respectively. The Roman numeral III indicates the largest size. $150-275 according to size.

An unusual frowning face of the Sarreguemines-type jugs (no. 8715). *Courtesy of "Marty"* $175-295

Though often sold as Sarreguemines, the jugs just shown were not made there. The Sarreguemines turquoise interior of the jug is much deeper compared with the light colored interior of the other jug.

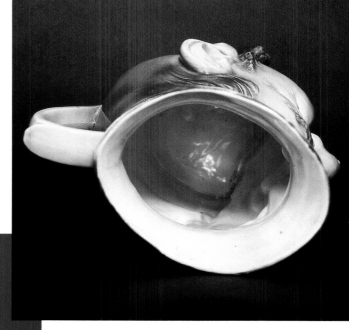

The rather sleepy look of these fellows gives them a certain charm (no. 8714). $100-275 according to size

The "green hat with pink bow" (no. 7890) . . .

. . . also came in monochrome. *Courtesy of M & G Bottero Antiquites, Nice* $100-295 according to size and coloring.

Often these jugs are described according to the hats they wear. "The black bill" (no. 7891) serves to describe this example. $100-250

Sometimes this jug is called "Matelot" (no. 7892) which is French for "sailor." The origin of the name is unknown and though its accuracy is questionable, collectors seem to recognize it. This jug came in five sizes, the smallest being 3" high. $75-295 according to size

This jug (no. 8716) is unusual. His flower gives him a comical air. $150-215

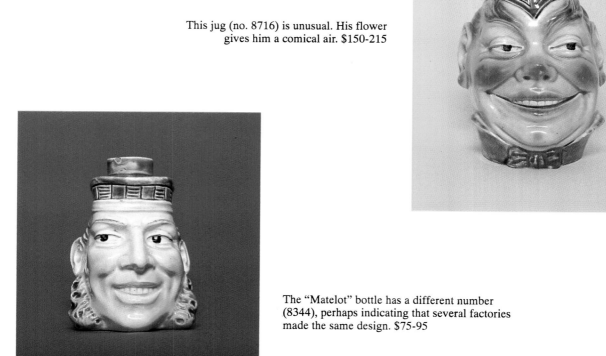

The "Matelot" bottle has a different number (8344), perhaps indicating that several factories made the same design. $75-95

The green hat with the black bill came with a variety of faces: frowning, smiling, with or without a cigar. 3" high. $65-85 each

Different factories or just different decorators? The skin tone varies considerably on these two jugs. $65-85

These rare 3" bottles are thicker potted than the other Sarreguemines-type jugs, perhaps indicating a different factory. One wonders if the cartoon-like appearance of all three perhaps indicates their origin. Perhaps popular puppet characters or storybook figures? Yellow hat (no.9988), monocle (no. 8863), Happy Hooligan-type figure (no.8863). $100-150 each

St. Clément

About 1723 Jacques Chambrette opened a studio in the Lunéville, then part of the old Duchy of Lorraine. The wonderful clay in the area was perfect for producing faïence. By 1749 the Chambrette factory became potters for the king of Poland. In order to sell his wares in France without an import tax, Chambrette opened a branch at St. Clément (pronounced San Cleh'mon) in 1758. The branch was situated in the Territory of the Three Bishoprics, an area that included Verdun, Metz, and Toul. This area was exempt from import taxes to France.

Chambrette's son-in-law, Charles Loyal, managed St. Clément along with Richard Mique, an architect, and Paul-Louis Cyfflé, a sculptor and modeler from Lunéville. Upon the death of Chambrette shortly after the opening of the St. Clément, Jacques's son Gabriel and Charles Loyal ran the factory. The firm began having financial difficulties, only to be liquidated. Loyal, Cyfflé, and Mique then purchased it. In 1788 the Sebastian Keller family and Guérin, their partner, purchased the Lunéville factory.

In 1824 Germain Thomas purchased St. Clément and in 1840 passed it on to his three sons. By 1892 the owners of Lunéville, Keller and Guérin, acquired St. Clément.

St. Clément, like several other French factories, manufactured majolica from Arnoux kilns purchased from Minton. The firm is known for its fine, subtle coloring perhaps because of the proximity of the famous French glass makers, Auguste and Antonin Daum and Émile Gallé, in the nearby city of Nancy. Gallé, in fact, worked at St. Clément in 1864.

Though the Lunéville factory closed as World War I began, it was reopened after the war when the Fenal family purchased it along with St. Clément in 1922.[18]

While Lunéville's majolica production specialized in asparagus plates and coffee services, St. Clément made some fine figures. These figures are known for their soft, gently blended coloring and glass-like appearance. Most, though not all, of the figures are marked with a low-relief superimposed "K" and "G" (Keller and Guérin) often with a similarly written "S" and "C" (St. Clément) on a white base. After World War I the name of the firm written in small black script came into use.

The animal jugs are tall (about 12" to 13") and generally rather narrow. The figures include dogs, parrots, pelicans, a seated monkey, cockatoos, a leopard, and a grasshopper which is rare. St. Clément made only four toby jugs and they are easily identifiable, even if unmarked. All are three-quarter figures in grayish tones with pinkish or white monotone faces. The four figures consist of Mireillé, Henry IV, Napoleon, and Joan of Arc.

St. Clément is reproducing a limited number of its animal figures, but the collector can readily distinguish them from the old models because of their colors and lack of detail. These pieces have a high gloss not seen on the old models, as well as more intense colors like lime greens and lemon yellows. The duck, parrot, cockatoo, and elephant are examples of new productions. All are marked with the name of the firm in small script.

The subtle coloring of this St. Clément rooster indicates age. The blue and yellow is reversed on another example from this period. More recent rooster jugs have brighter coloring. 14" high. *Courtesy of M & G Bottero Antiquites, Nice* $340-495

St. Clément duck jugs came in several sizes with the largest being 17" high. The most common size is around 13" high. *Courtesy of M & G Bottero Antiquites, Nice* $150-500 according to size.

Two ducks by St. Clément: The hatching duck jug is unique. The smaller duck is a bank from the 1930s, approximately 4" high. *Courtesy of Bertrand Cocq* $900-1,300 with egg; $100-145 bank.

Although colored like parrots, these St. Clément jugs are cockatoos because of their crest. (St. Clément made a parrot with a red head and no crest.) The tallest cockatoo, 15.5" high, is the oldest, circa 1880. The lighter coloring and the black beak with a hooked end indicate age. The middle cockatoo, 14" high, was made between 1900 and 1904 and is unmarked. The lack of detail in the feathers indicates a worn mold, since molds lost their definition with repeated use. The 13" duck on the left has the black mark and a straight blue (not black) beak: evidence that this jug was made after World War I. *Courtesy of Bertrand Cocq* $100-300 according to age.

This St. Clément marabou stork jug has a very small hole in its beak for the spout, perhaps indicating it was intended for absinthe. An exotic bird, the marabou is indigenous to Africa and southeast Asia. 12.25" high. *Courtesy of Bertrand Cocq* $500-700

Dogs have long been popular in ceramics. This bank by St. Clément was made during the 1930s. *Courtesy of Bertrand Cocq* $95-150

The cat jug by St. Clément sits on a plinth base. 12.25" high. *Courtesy of Bertrand Cocq* $395-495

On the collar the name "Gypp" appears. This whippet was made by St. Clément. *Courtesy of Leprechaun Antiques* $600-900

Two seated animal jugs by St. Clément include the pig on the barrel and the seated monkeys. The monkeys came on red and on green plinth bases. *Courtesy of Bertrand Cocq* $400-550 monkeys; $550-700 pig.

An elephant with a raised trunk means good luck according to an old superstition. This St. Clément elephant is seated like many of the animal jugs made by the firm. 10" high. *Courtesy of Bertrand Cocq* $400-550

The interest in the exotic is evident in this unusual leopard jug. St. Clément is one of the few firms to make a model of this animal. *Courtesy of Jacques Salzard* $600-750

St. Clément made a bank of Mr. Baudon. The more well-known Onnaing example of the same figure is a jug. *Courtesy of Jacques Salzard* $400-500

This St. Clément monk appears to be clutching his bottle. Monks are popular figures for jugs and flasks. *Courtesy of Henriette and Philippe Bailet* $250-400

St. Clément made four bust jugs in this series: Mireillé, Henry IV, Joan of Arc, and Napoleon. This example has "Jeanne d'Arc" written on her chest. *Courtesy of M & G Bottero Antiquites, Nice* $350-450

Napoleon was a popular figure for ceramic manufacturers, including St. Clément who made this jug. *Courtesy of Bertrand Cocq* $375-475

St. Clément also made the same series as banks. Napoleon and Joan of Arc seemed the most popular. *Courtesy of M & G Bottero Antiquites, Nice* $125-195

This smiling face seems appropriate for a St. Clément bank! 7" high.
Courtesy of M & G Bottero Antiquites, Nice $195-225

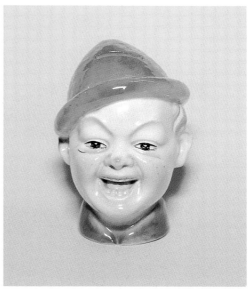

This St. Clément marmalade pot is most unique.
Courtesy of M & G Bottero Antiquites, Nice.
$250-350

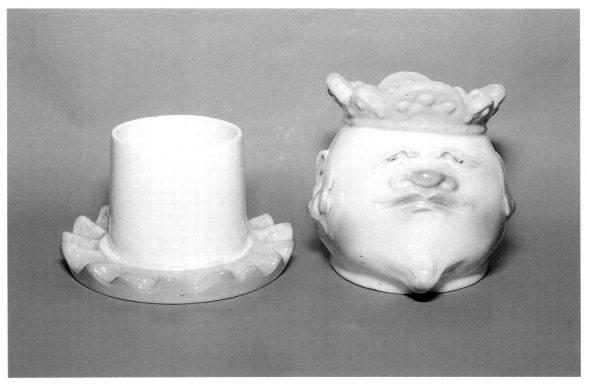

Nimy and Onnaing

The pottery factories of Nimy-les-Mons in Belgium and Onnaing (pronounced Nee'-mee and Oh'-naang respectively) in France lie along the same clay vein that runs from northern France across the Belgium border. The products of these two factories closely resemble each other in weight and coloring, but each factory had its own molds and designs.

In 1797 Charles, Knight of de Boursies, founded a small pottery firm called Faïencerie de Ferriere-la-Petite in Belgium. On March 7, one year later, he was joined by Frederick, Baron of Secus, in founding the Nimy firm.

Dranem, the popular comedian from the turn of the century, appeared as a toby jug for Nimy. The mark is in black ink. 13" high. $900-1,200

Nimy made a limited number of figures, including this owl. The red interior indicates its French origin, even though the figure is similar to the Staffordshire birds. *Courtesy of "collection touranqelle"* $400-500

This Nimy sailor jug has a red interior like many French jugs. *Courtesy of Gerri & Jim Trout* $450-565

In February of 1821, Charles and his two brothers, Adolphe and Ferdinand-Louis, along with Frederick opened a factory at Onnaing. Onnaing was situated near Valenciennes, just southeast of Lille, about twenty miles from the Belgium border.

About this same time the mayor of Nimy-les-Mons, Jean-Pierre Mouzin, acquired partial ownership and the directorship of the pottery factory in Nimy. By April 27, 1858, Jean-Pierre and his brother Jean-Baptiste also became administrators of Onnaing.

Jean-Baptiste Mouzin controlled Onnaing until 1870 at which time Jean Gerschwing-Mouzin took control. In 1884 Auguste Mouzin briefly managed Onnaing. Eugene Meyer-Mouzin became director from 1884 until 1886 and Edouard Mouzin managed Onnaing until 1893.

On March 14, 1894, Nimy and Onnaing combined to create the Onnaing Society under the directorship of Adolphe Lecat. Eugene Hans-Mouzin controlled both factories until 1919 at which time Charles Mouzin took control.[19]

Both factories rose to fame for their products of figures, in particular, toby jugs. The clay pipes of Scouflaire, located near Onnaing, served as inspiration for some of these jugs.

During World War I Onnaing manufactured only useful items like plates and utensils. In addition, they could import Bavarian porcelains cheaply, so they added these items to their sales. At this time people struggled merely to survive. Onnaing lay only fifty miles from the lines of battle, so fanciful items like majolica figurals did not sell. Majolica production ceased.

After the war Onnaing tried once more to produce majolica figures, but since the old molds had been destroyed during the war, new molds had to be made. Unfortunately, the new models did not sell well and finally in 1938 Onnaing ceased production completely.

Though Nimy and Onnaing figures are generally light weight and not as detailed as Sarreguemines pieces or many English figures, their subject matter and comical air make them highly collectible. Political subjects must have intrigued the potters at Onnaing, for they frequently took insignificant contemporary issues and made humorous toby jugs about them.

For example, in 1906 the French National Assembly asked one of its deputies of accounting, Mr. Auguste Baudon (1848-1913) from Oise, to prepare a study on whether all deputies needed a pay raise. In November of 1906 Mr. Baudon returned to the Assembly and with great flair reported that all deputies did indeed need a salary increase. In January of 1907, a raise from 10,000 to 15,000 French francs took effect. The irony of allowing a deputy within the organization to make an in-depth report on a raise did not escape the pottery designers at Onnaing and the previously unknown Mr. Baudon soon appeared as a toby jug![20]

Other humorous treatments included the drunken army reservist sitting astride a beer barrel or the pig dressed as the maitre d'hôtel. In addition to jovial pieces, Onnaing also made popular figures like Joan of Arc. Other figures included banks and tobacco jars. Onnaing figures have a deep burgundy interior.

The railroader and the miner are popular figures in the north of France, so these jugs attract gift-givers seeking a present for a relative who worked in one of those industries; consequently, these jugs are very hard to find. The uniform of the railroader is that of the Chemin de Fer du Nord, one of ten private companies that existed in France at the turn of the century. Eventually all railroads were nationalized.

Another hard to find jug by Onnaing is "La Madelon." Named after Mrs. Madelon who served food and sang to troops in World War I, the name came to represent anyone who served in that capacity. The term is one of endearment as she was the only woman the soldiers saw, and she was treated with respect.

The marks of Nimy include "Mouzin Freres" (brothers) or the names "Mouzin-Lecat" in a circle. Sometimes the names are followed by "& Cie." for "and company." Onnaing marks generally are "Frie O," short for Faïencerie d'Onnaing, with a crest in the middle. Older pieces have only a circle with three whisker-like lines on each side and a mold or design number.

Toby jugs by mold number:

808 Alsatian Woman with Braids
775 Railroader
762 Francisco Ferrer
451 King's Jester
758 Rooster, "le Gaulois-Chante Claire pour la France"
    or "Vive la Russie"
791 Joan of Arc
784 "Jupe Coulotte" (pant-skirt)
763 Marianne
799 "La Madelon"
789 Franco-Russian Alliance or "l'entente cordial"
797 Miner
826 Paul Déroulède
816 Poincaré
752 Army reservist
706 Monk
737 Hotel Manager
 36 Bulldog
741 Deputy (Mr.Baudon)
778 Dolphin
755 Pig with ham
712 Duck

Banks

881 Squirrel
882 Snail
460 Pigeon
798 Wild Boar
883 Frog
859 Cat
871 Basset
885 Chinaman
886 Man's head
887 Woman's head
892 Turtle

Tobacco Jars

804 Moroccan man
902 Laughing man

During World War I Onnaing made these rooster pitchers for children to canvas the neighborhoods seeking donations to help wounded soldiers. Ninety percent of all these pitchers have broken or restored beaks because the children often hit the door frame when they thrust the pitcher forward to receive the money. For the first two years of the war the phrase on the pitcher read, "Vive la Russie." After 1914, the patriotic phrase became, "Le Gaulois" on one side and "Chante clair pour la France" on the other. Chaunticleer was the rooster known for his beautiful voice in one of Geoffrey Chaucer's *Cantebury Tales*; the French phrase when translated reads "sing brightly for France." Puns such as this one appear on much of the French ceramics. *Courtesy of Bertrand Cocq* $250-$450 depending upon the phrase.

The Onnaing ducks came in two shades of green. Perhaps the "P.V." mark on the bottom represents an importer. Ducks are common food sources in France so they appear frequently in pottery designs, just as the chicken and the pig do. *Courtesy of Bertrand Cocq* $225-350

Onnaing, like many other manufacturers of the time, made a gurgling fish pitcher. *Courtesy of M & G Bottero Antiquities, Nice* $395-495

The Onnaing pig waiters had either brown or gray jackets. *Courtesy of Bertrand Cocq* $450-550

This bulldog was one of the last pieces of majolica made by Onnaing just before they discontinued production for the second time. Only a limited number were made. $650-775

Onnaing made a line of figural banks, all of which are around 3.5" high. *Courtesy of Bertrand Cocq* $120-190 each.

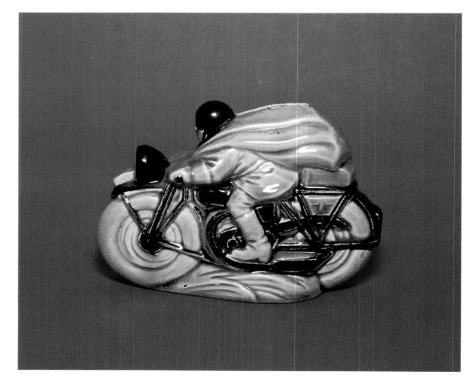

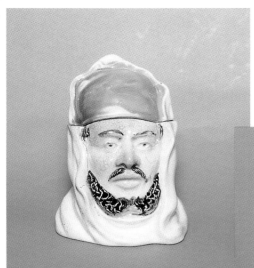

The miner was a common figure in the north of France, a region known for its coal mines. Though not especially rare, the Onnaing miner is hard to find because it is cross-collected. *Courtesy of "Marty"* $500-600

Onnaing also made a bank of a Moroccan figure, as did many other continental manufacturers. 6.5" high. *Courtesy of M & G Bottero Antiquities, Nice* $250-325

The "fou de roi" or king's jester is one of the few character jugs made by Onnaing. 7.5" high. *Courtesy of Bertrand Cocq* $475-600

The Onnaing railroader is another jug that is cross-collected. Note the deep burgundy interior, typical of all Onnaing jugs. $500-650

The Onnaing monk and his mark. $225-275

Onnaing immortalized Raymond Poincaré who was the president of France from 1913 to 1920. The back of the jug closely resembles that of the railroader jug. (A similarly styled jug represented Francisco Ferrer, the Spanish anarchist.) $395-495

Paul Déroulède, the president of a patriotic league in 1882 and known for his patriotic poems and songs prior to World War I, appeared in pottery by Onnaing. $395-495

The Onnaing drunken army reservist astride a barrel better hope he is not called to action! $400-495

Deputy Baudon reported to the French National Assembly in 1906 that each deputy did indeed need a pay raise to 15,000 francs. Onnaing mocked this contemporary event in pottery. $400-495

The liberation movement for women (called the "MLF" or "movement de liberation de la femme" in France) perhaps wore "la jupe-coulotte" similar to this one created for Onnaing by Victor Alglave. Designers at Onnaing often used contemporary events as inspiration for their pottery. This model also appeared with a gray-green hat. 12" high. Note the Art Nouveau curving lines reminiscent of Louis XV. *Courtesy of "Marty"* $495-675

Onnaing manufactured this patriotic jug called "Marianne" for only about ten years because it was not particularly popular. $450-600

Representing the Franco-Russian alliance at the time of World War I, when the czar of Russia visited the Dunkerque area, this Onnaing jug depicts a French woman wearing the skin of a bear, the symbol for Russia. Known as "l'entente cordial," the jug is sometimes called "Peau d'âne" because of the similarity to the French children's story. That name seems inaccurate, however, since the skin in the story is that of a donkey, not a bear. *Courtesy of Bertrand Cocq* $550-650

This jug by Onnaing is an Alsatian woman with braids. The mark here has only the "O" and not the entire name. $450-600

The Onnaing version of Joan of Arc resembles the one by St. Clément but is more colorful with more detail. *Courtesy of Jacques Salzard* $500-600

Orchies and the Moulin des Loups

In 1879 Emile Lhermine opened a pottery works at Rimbaud in Belgium, a location famous for pottery since the Middle Ages. The factory had an auspicious beginning and by 1886 Lhermine realized a need to enlarge the production area. He and his brothers bought an old textile factory and expanded their production with the addition of three new kilns.

Continually enlarging the production and hiring an enameler, the Lhermine brothers opened a branch in Orchies, France, not far from the Belgium border. The mark at this time consisted of an impressed windmill (moulin in French) with "Orchies" in block letters underneath.

At this time forty-eight Belgium families emigrated to Orchies and aided in the production of faïence. By 1910 the factory employed 175 workers.

In neighboring St. Amand-les-Eaux, the pottery factory merged with the factory of Hamages to form the Moulin des Loups & Hamage. In 1923 Orchies purchased them and included their names. The black mark consisted of a windmill inside a circle of the three names.

During this period Orchies (pronounced Or'-shee) specialized in table services and utilitarian wares, but continued to develop its productions and later added hand-painted luxury items. They exported to Austria, Switzerland, Italy, and Belgium, as well as to French colonies.

From 1950 to 1970, the Orchies factory employed 550 workers, 60% of them women. After nearly 100 years of operation, the factory at Orchies closed its doors in 1988. In 1992 the site was razed to make way for a new department store. Only the old smoke stacks remain.[21]

Around the turn of the century Orchies produced approximately twenty majolica figural jugs, most of them full-figured animals on their haunches. Only four models of toby jugs are known to exist and two of these are three-quarter figures of people. Generally the jugs are marked with one or two letters, often indicating the French word for the figure. For example, the rabbit pitcher is marked "LP." Lapin is the French word for the animal. Somewhat dully colored, these figural jugs are generally well executed and quite appealing.

A list of figural jugs includes:

ZV Zouave (Name of the French soldiers fighting in
    North Africa)
CP Dog (chien in French)
 Z Cat Playing the Mandolin
AG Frog Hunter (grenouille)
CY Swan (cygne)
PL Pelican
PC Policeman
SP Fireman (Sapeur-Pompier)
CR Duck (canard)
CH Cabbage (choux) with a child's face for spout
AE Squirrel (écureuil)
EB Rooster
KL Cat on haunches
LP Rabbit
RF Fox (renard)
AD Hen

With the exception of the mandolin playing cat and the duck, few of these figural jugs are being reproduced.

The Orchies cat playing the mandolin appeared with two different eye colors: yellow and green. Note the rather dull colors as opposed to the brighter colors on the reproductions now being made. *Courtesy of Bertrand Cocq* $395-450

The Orchies pig, made around 1910, resembles one discontinued by Onnaing. Orchies marked its jugs with one or two letters and sometimes a number. Pork accounts for a large part of the French diet in the northern areas, so pigs appear frequently in French ceramic designs. 8.5" high. *Courtesy of M & G Bottero Antiquites, Nice* $385-450

This Orchies cat, like the one playing the mandolin, has green eyes. *Courtesy of Bertrand Cocq* $475-535

This Orchies braying donkey seems very stubborn! *Courtesy of Bertrand Cocq* $500-600

Orchies made several models of domestic birds like these roosters and the duck. The taller rooster is 12" high; the shorter is 9" high. *Courtesy of Bertrand Cocq* $500-650 each

Animals like the city badger with his umbrella, 8.75" high, and the rabbits with their carrots are by Orchies. The rabbit, 9.25" high, with the white carrot is rare, while the ones with orange carrots are slightly more common. *Courtesy of Bertrand Cocq* $395-495.

The Orchies frog hunter came in two sized jugs, 10" and 9" high. The snake acts as the handle. *Courtesy of Bertrand Cocq* $495-650

The Orchies dog climbing out of the barrel is unique. *Courtesy of Jacques Salzard.* $600-695

The Orchies squirrel with the blue interior is rare. Most of the squirrels have a burgundy interior. The jug came in three different sizes. *Photography by Jill Graham* $700-900

"Coree" means Korea, and the Russian bear is attacking Korea. This Orchies jug has the initials "RJ" on the bottom. *Courtesy of Bertrand Cocq* $550-650

Orchies made four three-quarter figures. The Zouave, "ZV" on the base of the jug, is the name for the French soldiers fighting in North Africa. 10.25" high. The "SP" or "Sapeur-Pompier" means fireman. Both are hard to find. *Courtesy of Bertrand Cocq* $800-1,000 each

The student jug by Orchies has a signature of the designer on the side: Foubert. *Courtesy of M & G Bottero Antiquites, Nice* $600-900

The automobilist by Orchies. *Courtesy of Jacques Salzard* $700-1,000

The Massiers

The Massier brothers (pronounced Mah'-see-aa), Delphin (born in 1836) and Clément (1845-1917), along with their cousin Jérôme (born in 1850) began a pottery operation in 1862 on the French Riviera. As tourists returned from Africa they visited the Riviera, so the location was perfect for a pottery enterprise. Delphin and Jérôme worked in Vallauris, while Clément had his shop in nearby Golfe-Juan. Jacques and Elisabeth, parents of the brothers, had been potters since the early nineteenth century and it was Elisabeth who created the intense turquoise glaze which was to become the trademark of Clément. Delphin achieved fame with his animals ranging in size from 2.5" to 3'. Jérôme utilized small scale designs, including singing frogs, which delight collectors today.

The Massiers began majolica production in 1860. Known for their highly glazed, strikingly colored majolica, they hired many-well known artists to work at the factory. Perhaps the best known was Lucien Lévy. After working with Clément from 1887-1895, Lévy became one of the leading artists of the Art Nouveau movement, painting under the name Lévy-Dhurmer. Other artists included Jean Barol and Jacques Sicard, both known for their iridescent glazes. Sicard was later to work in the United States at Weller Pottery where he introduced a line of art pottery called Sicardo. These pieces are highly collected today.

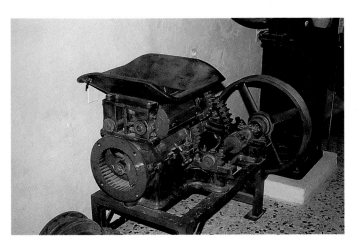

Examples of the old equipment used in Vallauris at the Massiers factory still remain there in a museum. The cart for transporting the clay, machines for breaking the stones and mixing the clay, the old filter-presses, and the kiln entrance illustrate the real labor involved in making pottery during the nineteenth century. *Courtesy of Musée de la Poterie, Vallauris*

The Massiers experimented with color, creating an entirely new palette for majolica by using the reduction technique. A reduction atmosphere in a kiln is one low in oxygen and high in carbon dioxide. By reglazing a piece with copper oxide and refiring it, a profound range of colors appeared.

By the turn of the century the Massier firm was the largest employer in the area. Clément rose to fame using his mother's wonderful turquoise glaze. Elisabeth had traveled to the neighboring town of Grasse, known for its delightful perfumes. There she gathered copper oxide by scraping the sides of the stills for making perfumes and used these oxides to make her uniquely subtle, yet rich turquoise glaze. Clément was also aided by Gandolfo Gaetano, who understood the Hispano-Moresque methods.[22]

Ancient Persians believed that turquoise would ward off evil spirits, so Persian wares of the twelfth and thirteenth centuries were richly glazed in this color. The Victoria and Albert Museum has a wonderful display of these monochromatic Persian wares. Through the centuries this color has continued to attract the attention of potters. The Minton and the Sarreguemines turquoise differs slightly from the Massier color. By examining the turquoise used by each of these factories, it becomes possible to distinguish between them.

Clément made few figures, but became known for his large pieces, especially the jardinieres and pedestals. Using only one color or gently blending two colors is a trademark of Clément. The muted reds with deep greens merging, much as the Impressionists merged colors, make it easy to identify Clément's work from that of his brother and cousin.

Delphin established a reputation for his wonderful creatures like the grasshopper, flamingo, cat, pig, and rooster. Jérôme also made roosters, along with a series of small frogs. Masterfully crafted, all of these animals attracted the attention of the royalty and upper class sophisticates who vacationed on the Riviera in the late nineteenth century. They carried or shipped home pieces of the Massiers' majolica which spread the firm's fame quickly. This fame, however, did not keep the factory from closing shortly after the turn of the century.

The most well-known of Delphin's animals are perhaps his life-size flamingos and his roosters with their bright, highly glazed ochres, cadmium reds, and burnt siennas, colors associated with Impressionist paintings. The incredible sunlight of the south of France attracted the Impressionist painters who wanted to experiment with color. It is easy to understand the association between them and the potters in the area.

Although many Massiers pieces are unmarked, their glossy, intensely colored glazes, make attribution possible. Many pieces are signed, however. Clément's pieces are impressed with his name and the name of the city. Delphin signed his pieces in black with his name and "Vallauris, France A. M." for Alpes-Marine, the region of France. Jérôme's pieces are impressed with "Jérôme Massier, Fils" (Jerome Massier, Junior) and the city's name within an oval. In general collectors consider figures by Clément and Delphin as slightly more important than the pieces by their cousin.

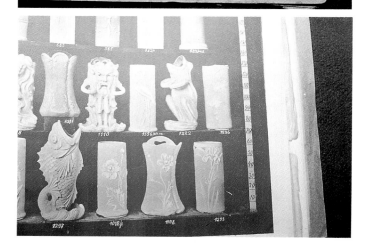

Opposite page photos:
The Massier catalog from 1908 offered combinations of colors as well as a variety of models including the frog pitcher and bird figurines. *Courtesy of Robert Lehr*

The flambé seen in the Massier catalog appears on the comb of this rooster egg cup. *Courtesy of M & G Bottero Antiquites, Nice* $450-550

Delphin Massier made this realistic cat. 5.75" high by 10" long. *Courtesy of Anne Ford Associates, Inc.* $3,000-$4,000

This wonderful grasshopper planter displays the unusual chartreuse used by Delphin Massier. 10" high by 19.5" long. *Courtesy of Anne Ford Associates, Inc.* $8,000-9,000

A Massier tortoise 2.5" high. *Courtesy of M & G Bottero Antiquites, Nice* $500-595

The Massier chartreuse appears on this unique frog jug with a frog handle by Delphin. *Courtesy of M & G Bottero Antiquites, Nice* $1,400-1,700

This pig appeared as a toothpick holder and as a figurine in the turquoise created by Elisabeth Massier. 3.5" high. *Courtesy of M & G Bottero Antiquites, Nice* $550-600 each

This little elephant planter is only 3.5" tall. *Courtesy of M & G Bottero Antiquites, Nice* $300-500

This bull figurine resembles one made by Sarreguemines. 6.75" high. *Courtesy of M & G Bottero Antiquites, Nice* $550-675

The burro also appeared with gray baskets instead of yellow. 19" high. *Courtesy of Anne Ford Associates, Inc.* $5,000-6,000

This unique Arab head is a 4" wall plaque. *Courtesy of M & G Bottero Antiquites, Nice* $600-850

Old postcards showing the interior and the exterior of the Jérôme Massier showroom in Vallauris, France. *Courtesy of M & G Bottero Antiquites, Nice*

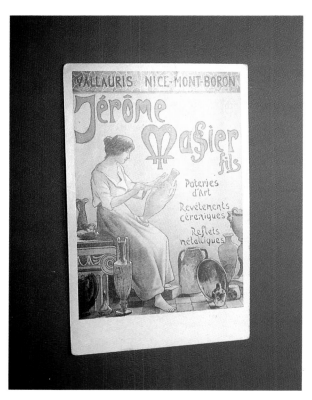

An old postcard of an advertisement for Jérôme Massier, Fils, Pottery. *Courtesy of M & G Bottero Antiquites, Nice*

The site of the old firm still exists, but today houses private offices. *Courtesy of M & G Bottero Antiquites, Nice*

Jérôme Massier, Fils, made a variety of small frogs which are highly collectible. Some are signed with an impressed mark, while others carry only the signature with and without the entire first name. From 2.5 to 4.5" high. *Courtesy of M & G Bottero Antiquites, Nice* $475-850

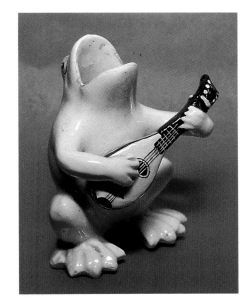

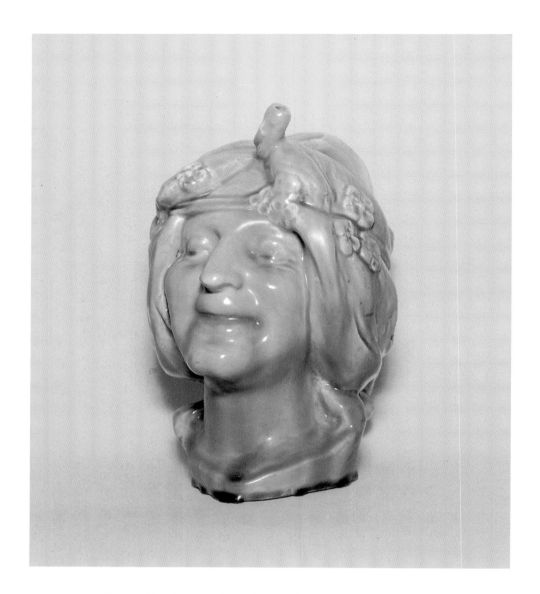

Clément Massier generally made large pieces like jardinieres and
pedestals and only a few figures. This face may represent his mother
who created the distinctive turquoise glaze for which he became
known. *Courtesy of M & G Bottero Antiquites, Nice* $1,000-1,500

DELPHIN MASSIER.
VALLAURIS. (A.M.)

Clement-Massier

J. Massier Fils.
Vallauris

Chapter Six

French Firms:
Limited Productions of Figures

Desvres

Little information is available about the manufacture of majolica at Desvres (pronounced Deh' vruh), a center primarily known for its faïence. A few majolica figures exist, but they are extremely rare and are included for informational purposes only. Usually the pieces are comical with muddy coloring and with little attention to detail. Thickness in potting and a slightly heavier feel indicate the possibility of Desvres.

The faïencerie was founded in 1760 by Jean François Sta. In 1802 his son sold the factory. François-Joseph Fourmentraux, born in Lille in 1764, worked at

Desvres in 1791, but in 1804 he left to start his own factory at Fives, a suburb of Lille. Sta's three sons took control of Desvres, one after another. Sta died in 1885, but Louis-François and his brothers continued to run the factory. Louis-François died in 1885 and his son Jules managed Desvres until 1887.

In 1903 François Masse bought the factory, and it was during this time that a few majolica figures were manufactured. Marguerite Masse continued to direct the operation of Desvres after her husband died. Eventually their son Robert took control.[1]

Desvres majolica is marked "FM" presumably for François Masse, though it has been suggested that they stand for Fourmentraux and Masse. The initials appear within a shield-shaped outline. Desvres figures include an elephant smoking a pipe, as well as the ones pictured in this chapter.

Desvres figures have a heavier feel and muddy coloring. They are marked with "FM" in a shield. All Desvres figurals are extremely rare. *Courtesy of Bertrand Cocq* Rare

This Desvres soldier is one of the few human figures made by the firm. *Courtesy of Jacques Salzard* Rare

Fives-Lille

Jean Bernard De Bruyn, born in 1745 in Anvers, Belgium, opened a pottery works at Louvain. He died in 1805. His son Martin, born in 1777, operated the factory until his son Denis De Bruyn, who was born in 1804, took control.

Denis' son Antoine Gustave De Bruyn, born in 1838, moved to Lille and opened a pottery firm around 1862. Gustave lived at 20 rue de Juliers in Fives, a suburb, with his wife and two children. Called "Little Belgium" because of the large population of immigrant workers, Fives had been annexed to Lille four years earlier.

Gustave moved to 18 rue de Malakoff and eventually to rue de l'Esperance where he built a factory next to his house. In 1879 the De Bruyn factory included stonewares and earthenwares in its catalog. Six years later bricks and tiles were added. In 1887 "barbotines décorées" wares appeared in the catalog. Barbotine is the French word for the powder used in making clay, and the word is applied to faïence and majolica pieces generally with very thin, high relief flowers or decoration. From 1905 until 1938 the word "majolique" appeared in the catalog.

In 1889 the De Bruyn firm received the gold medal at the Universal Exhibition in Paris, as well as a prize of 1,000 francs from La Société Industrielle du Nord for the introduction of a new industry, artistic pottery, into the Nord department (or region) of France. Two years later, Gustave left Lille, nearly thirty years after his arrival. The firm employed 150 workers at that time.

Gustave's sons entered the business and the firm name became De Bruyn & Sons. Just before World War I the factory employed 400 workers, but a fire in 1917, one year after De Bruyn's death, destroyed one of the chimneys and a great deal of the supplies, causing much disorganization.

By 1927 the name became just De Bruyn Sons, but the economic crisis between the wars caused a great deal of conflict between workers and management. The wares at this time changed to become brighter, more angular, and more animated. Stereotypical characters associated with the era appeared.

In 1950 the factory consisted of three sections, one of which was the artistic faïence. All three sections were sold that year, with the artistic division going to Raymond Henri Chevalier for the sum of 6,500 francs. He died on July 21, 1959, and the factory closed on April 18, 1962.[2] Included in their products are approximately eight to ten figural pitchers and banks.

"La Mere Michelle" is a pitcher of a woman crying because she has lost her cat, designed after a children's song of the same name. The cat is poking his head under the hem of Michelle's dress in the back. Another well-known piece from Fives-Lille is "Je Sais Tout" or "I know everything." Given away as a premium to purchasers of an entire set of encyclopedias, the pitcher or bank depicts a man whose head is shaped like a world globe. Since each volume of the encyclopedia had a letter on the spine, they spelled "Je Sais Tout" when all together. It was possible to purchase one volume at a time, so the encyclopedia company offered a premium to those who bought the entire set together.

Other familiar figurals include the pipe-smoking frog, the policeman with the figure of a thief as the handle, and a serving dish shaped like a fish. With the invention of the automobile, stereotypes of motorists appeared in pottery. The "automobilist" in a brown coat and black hat with a rose-colored neck scarf covering his face so that only his eyes show seemed to offer a humorous version of an everyday scene. The model also appeared as a woman in tan-colored driving attire. This piece has a pink interior.

Another stereotypical figure is the drunken guard of the hunt, pictured as a pitcher. A tree trunk forms his handle and the figure slouches forward so that his hat forms the spout. Banks were made in similar figures. In addition "the drunken woman" became a pitcher.

The De Bruyn firm mark consists of the initials "D" and "B" superimposed over an anchor. Now pieces from this factory are simply called "Fives-Lille" (pronounced Feev-Leel).

Fives-Lille listed this fish serving dish in their catalog. *Courtesy of Leprechaun Antiques* $750-900

The pipe-smoking frogs by Fives-Lille appeared with four different colored coats: green, blue, red, brown. *Courtesy of Bertrand Cocq* $500-625

"Je Sais Tout" appeared by Fives-Lille as a premium (both as a jug and as a tobacco jar) for purchasers of an entire set of encyclopedias by the same name, which means "I know everything." 9.75" high. *Courtesy of Bertrand Cocq* $500-700

The small child is a bank by Fives-Lille approximately 4" high. *Courtesy of Bertrand Cocq* $145-195

Fives-Lille also made this hunter tobacco jar. 7.5" high. *Courtesy of Bertrand Cocq* $175-250

"La Mere Michelle" by Fives-Lille represents a children's story about a woman who is crying because she has lost her cat. The cat is poking its head from under her dress in the back. *Courtesy of Bertrand Cocq* $500-700

George Dreyfus

In 1890 George Dreyfus opened a small works at Moret-sur-Loing, south of Paris. He opened a shop in Paris on the rue de Paradis. The Dreyfus line included figures in the shapes of cats, chickens, dogs, fish, and bears. Other items included majolica given away as premiums for the Amieux canned food company.

Dreyfus marked his wares with his initials, sometimes inside a square representing a calling card with the corner turned down in accordance with calling card customs of the day.[3]

George Dreyfus made this chicken salt cellar marked "GD" within a calling card design. 2.75" high. *Courtesy of M & G Bottero Antiquites, Nice* $400-500

The automobilist was a common figure around the turn of the century when these jugs were made by Fives-Lille. The companion piece (not shown here) is a man in a brown coat with a scarf hiding the lower half of his face. *Courtesy of Bertrand Cocq* $650-950

The popular cockatoo design did not escape Dreyfus who made this brightly colored jug. *Courtesy of Pam Ferrazzutti Antiques, Toronto* $625-695

Emile Tessier

In 1747 Jean-Loiseau of Touraine opened a firm in Malicorne, which is situated on the Sarthe River northwest of Tour. In 1829 the factory sold to Charles Cador who became partners with Jules Béatrix, Loiseau's son-in-law. Most of Malicorne's faïence depicted designs similar to other factories in the area.

With the arrival of Léon Pouplard in 1865, the factory acquired a distinctive style. Pouplard married Marie-Angèle Béatrice, granddaughter of Jules, and took control of the factory in 1890. He began using Breton motifs like those popular on Quimper. Signed with "PB" or "PBX," the mark and the wares appeared similar to those of Quimper. Sued by Quimper, Pouplard lost the suit and was forced to destroy his wares with the Breton motif.

Around 1898 Emile Tessier (pronounced Teh'-see-aa) apprenticed to Pouplard. In 1924 he opened a factory of his own with his brother-in-law Laze, but two years later, they parted. By 1940 the Tessier factory employed ninety-nine workers, producing faïence similar to other factories. One of the most important in the area, the factory marked its wares with a "T" and "E" joined at an angle from the bottom.

Odette, the second daughter of Emile, married Roger Desprès in 1929. Their son managed the factory until 1984 when a Metz businessman, Victor Deschang, purchased it.[4]

Tessier is included in this text because of several highly collectible toby jug designs made presumably in the 1930s or 1940s. These figures are part of many majolica figural and toby jug collections. The deep gold monochromic faces on these charming jugs have indistinct features. Representing French stereotypes from the early twentieth century, these comical jugs are thickly modeled and quite humorous. The figures rest on a green plinth base.

One jug depicts a man astride a barrel with the numbers "0-20-100-0." In French these numbers sound like the French phrase, "Oh, wine without water." Other figures include the "tenue garance" and the "gendarme." The gendarme acted as the sheriff for the town or village. His responsibilities included controlling unruly or misbehaving children.

The Tessier factory experienced financial difficulties like so many other pottery manufacturers. Though it still produces pottery, most for export to the United States, the factory only employs twelve workers. The mark remains the same.

The red and blue uniform worn by the French soldiers during the first two years of World War I was called "tenue garance" named after the garance, a red flower found in France. By 1916 the disadvantages of the red in the uniform were becoming obvious, so the red was omitted and the "bleu horizon" or "blue as the sky" uniform appeared. Emile Tessier modeled this jug as a French soldier. $355-425

An old postcard depicting the gendarme reprimanding a misbehaving child. *Courtesy of Bertrand Cocq*

The "gendarme" is a well-known French figure from before the first World War. The figure represents a local law enforcement officer for the towns, much like a sheriff. Tessier signed these jugs with his initials. $355-425

The French love of puns is evident on this jug by Tessier. When read in French the numbers on the jug sound like the French phrase for "Oh, wine without water." *Courtesy of M & G Bottero Antiquites, Nice* $350-425

Chapter Seven

Other Manufacturers of Figures

German

Not many of the German manufacturers of majolica who marked their products made figures. However, the Hugo Lonitz factory in Haldensleben, founded in 1868, marked their majolica with two fish within a circle. Between 1886 and 1904 the firm added "& Co." to its name.

Bird on a twig shelf ornament (no. 1576) by Hugo Lonitz. 6.75" high. *Britannia, Grays Antique Market, London* $800-1,200

Hugo Lonitz of Neuhaldensleben, Saxony made some nicely detailed centerpieces like this one with quail (no. 1204) 13" high. *Britannia, Grays Antique Market, London* $2,200-2,600

A wall pocket resembling a bird's nest with oak leaves and a finch by Hugo Lonitz. 8.25" high. *Britannia, Grays Antique Market, London* $1,600-2,000

Hugo Lonitz made this boy holding a shell centerpiece (no. 378). 11.25" high. *Britannia, Grays Antique Market, London* $700-1,100

Josef Strnact made a number of humidors. For more information on the factory, see the section entitled "Variations on a Theme."

Josef Strnact made this tobacco jar. *Courtesy of Everett Grist* $145-175

Bohemian

The Wilhelm Schiller & Sohns (Sons) factory produced ornate, somber wares in Bodenbach which is now Padmokly. Begun in the early 1820s as Schiller & Gerbing, the company split in 1885 into Gerbing and Stephan, and W. Schiller & Sohns. The latter's marks on majolica include the impressed initials "W S & S" either alone or within a cartouche. Gerbing & Stephan became F. & S. Gerbing from 1898 until 1905 when Alexander Gerbing took control.[1]

Wilhelm Schiller and Sohns (Sons) made this wonderful caparisoned elephant centerpiece with a unique howdah during the 1870s when the interest in exotic appealed to consumers. The mark consists of "W S & S" impressed. 21.25" high. *Courtesy of Anne Ford Associates, Inc.* $4,500-5,100

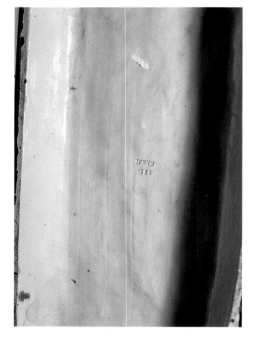

These Schiller wall plaques are hard to find in pairs. 14.5" high by 17.5" long. *Photography by Jill Graham* $1000-1500 pair

This exotic ostrich with a lady and child is a jardiniere and pedestal. 23.25" high. *Courtesy of Anne Ford Associates, Inc.* $4,500-5,100

This monkey and snake teapot was made by José A. Cunha at Caldas. 9" high. *Courtesy of Majolica Auctions by Michael G. Strawser* $475-575

W.S. & S.

Portuguese

Mannuel Cypriano Gomex Mafra manufactured majolica in Caldas de Rainha (Queen's bath) beginning in 1853. Mafra's son Cipriano Gomez Mafra took control is 1897. The firm manufactured toby jugs, as well as figurals and reptile ware similar to Palissy ware. The firm marked its wares with "Mafra" and an anchor underneath. "Caldas" appeared below the anchor. After 1890, the name of the country appeared below the name of the city. José Alves Cunha of Caldas also manufactured figurals, in particular, rather grotesque teapots.

A praying lizard made at Caldas. 13.25" high. *Courtesy of Bertrand Cocq* $500-750

Mafra at Caldas made a large gurgling fish not unlike the Staffordshire ones. The small mark was used around the turn of the century. 14.25" high. *Courtesy of M & G Bottero Antiquites, Nice* $575-725

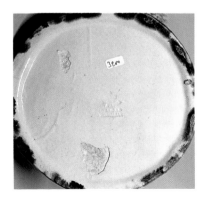

A unique toby jug with a hair braid as a handle. Made at Caldas. 11.25" high. $500-750

A bust jug by Mafra at Caldas with the small impressed mark. 9" high. $250-325

Very few American manufacturers made figures. George Morley, an English potter, came to America, and after working for other firms eventually opened his own shop in 1879 in Wellsville, Ohio. He opened a second location when he purchased the Lincoln Pottery Works of East Liverpool, Ohio, in the mid-1880s. The firm marked their products with "Morley & Co." below which appeared "Majolica" (sometimes spelled with two Ls) and the name of the respective city. Morley & Co. made a gurgling fish not unlike the Staffordshire designs, but the American version has a much rounder body with browns rather than grays in coloring.

This "ordinary toby" is an unusual piece, probably Portuguese. *Courtesy of Vic Schuler* $500-600

Though the American majolica makers rarely made figures, this unusual version of the gurgling fish appeared on the market by Morley and Company. 9" high. *Courtesy of Majolica Auctions by Michael G. Strawser* $195-255

Other pieces often attributed to American factories include pug pitchers which were made in several sizes. Some of these pieces are heavier than others of the same size. Whether some are English and some are American remains unknown. Some pugs and some bear pitchers have an impressed marking: "U. S. design patent pending." This mark indicates that the factory wanted to patent the design in the United States, but it does not necessarily mean that an American firm sought the patent. English manufacturers could seek a design patent to market the design in the United States.

Chapter Eight

Unattributed Majolica Figures

Probably English

Majolica pieces identified as "probably English" generally fall into animal categories: birds, dogs, fish, and monkeys. All have a relatively similar feel which is generally a little lighter than comparably sized French pieces. English pieces often include grays, browns, and blues (especially dull ultramarines) along with rose or sometimes green accent colors.

Birds, especially owls, must have appealed to the nineteenth-century consumer. This gray owl was probably made in Staffordshire. *Courtesy of Leprechaun Antiques* $300-425

These Staffordshire owls appeared in several sizes ranging from 11.25 to 7.25" high. *Courtesy of Majolica Auctions by Michael G. Strawser* $295-450

This resting peacock is a shelf ornament. *Courtesy of Leprechaun Antiques* $150-200

The three storks surround a spill vase. *Courtesy of Leprechaun Antiques.* $350-425

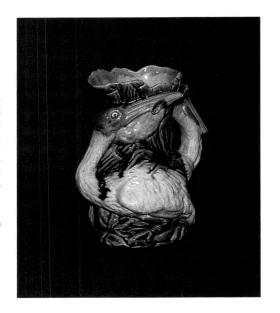

A jug with pelicans; the neck of one serves as the handle. 7.5" high. *Courtesy of Majolica Auctions by Michael G. Strawser* $500-600

A pair of unusual monkey candleholders. $700-950

The cello this dog jug holds makes it unique, since similar jugs usually appeared without one. $400-500

The monkey with bamboo jug came in several sizes. This example is 8" high. *Courtesy of Majolica Auctions by Michael G. Strawser* $300-500

These pug jugs vary in size and weight. Probably English, but some may have been made in America. *Courtesy of Gerri and Jim Trout* $300-500

A variety of fish jugs appeared on the market, not just the gurgling fish. These 4-sided fish with fish handles came in several sizes. *Courtesy of Majolica Auctions by Michael G. Strawser $225-350*

The Staffordshire fish swallowing fish teapot also came in a creamer design. $400-500 teapot; $200-295 creamer.

A frog on melon pitcher. Similar designs were made by several English manufacturers. *Courtesy of Majolica Auctions by Michael G. Strawser $650-850*

Ram pitchers with little detailing like these ranged in height from 8.5" to 9.5" high. *Courtesy of Majolica Auctions by Michael G. Strawser $100-165*

Probably French

French majolica, in general, has a slightly heavier feel than English pieces. In addition, pieces made in France have a colored interior, usually deep burgundy or turquoise. Deep burgundy interiors are rare on majolica made elsewhere.

A small swan planter with only the raised numbers 2089. 4.5" high. *Courtesy of M & G Bottero Antiques, Nice* $125-175

Two chickens, one a bank 4.25" high and the other a jug 8.5" high. *Courtesy of Bertrand Cocq* $125-165 bank; $200-300 jug.

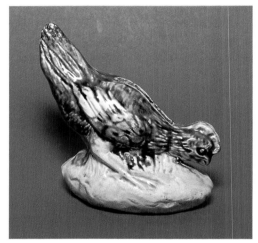

This raven pitcher has the burgundy interior typical of French jugs. *Courtesy of Leprechaun Antiques* $550-650

A rooster wall pocket almost 5" high. *Courtesy of Leprechaun Antiques* $250-400

A rooster jug in slightly different coloring. *Courtesy of Bertrand Cocq* $225-325

A small hen planter 2.75" high. *Courtesy of M & G Bottero Antiquites, Nice* $100-$150

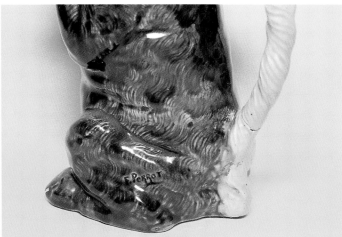

The dog pitcher has an unidentified low-relief butterfly mark on the underside of the base. The mark resembles one used by an importer, but is part of the mold. The dog is signed "F. Perrot" on the haunches. *Courtesy of Bertrand Cocq* $350-450

This "King Charles" dog jug and the cat with their similar coloring appear to be from the same manufacturer. Circa 1900. *Courtesy of M & G Bottero Antiquites, Nice* $375-475 each

Pigs were made in all sizes, from a small figurine to a large planter. *Courtesy of M & G Bottero Antiquites, Nice* $95-150 small; $200-300 large.

Two jugs praising the pig as a food source. The brown pig's phrase reads "Tout en est bon de la tete a la queue" or "all is good from the head to the tail." 10" high. The duck and pig are important in the French diet. Only a small portion of the duck is edible compared to the entire pig. The green and pink jug has sausage hanging from his shoulders. 9.5" high. *Courtesy of Bertrand Cocq* $400-500 each

A green pig pitcher. *Courtesy of M & G Bottero Antiquites, Nice* $300-400

This small pig figurine is enjoying his dinner. 2.5" high. $100-150

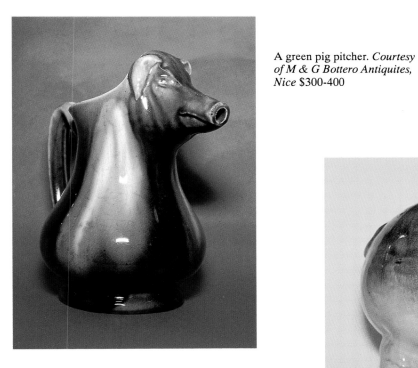

This large pig figurine is 9" high by 18" long. Though unmarked it possibly was made by Massier. *Courtesy of M & G Bottero Antiquites, Nice* $350-450

This small fish planter has the usual Massier turquoise, but not the weight. 2.5" high. *Courtesy of M & G Bottero Antiquites, Nice* $75-125

This unusual monkey pitcher has a scarf and a belt. Mocking man? *Courtesy of Bertrand Cocq* $295-395

A figural fish whose mouth is wider than the English models. 10" high. *Courtesy of Bertrand Cocq* $300-400

This unique fish is brighter colored than most others. The intense movement attracts the eye. *Courtesy of Roger Barbat* $300-450

A frog climbing into a shell which perhaps serves as a condiment dish. 4" high. *Courtesy of M & G Bottero Antiquites, Nice* $300-450

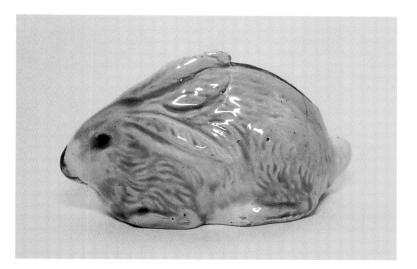

This small rabbit bank was possibly made by Massier but is unmarked. 3" high. *Courtesy of M & G Bottero Antiquites, Nice* $400-500

The bear with the stick jug has a burgundy interior. It was probably made in the Alps region of France where traveling bear shows entertained the townspeople. The trainer carried a stick in case the bear became dangerous, but here the bear is carrying the stick! 8.5" high. $375-475

Another version of the bear jug shows the animal carrying a tambourine. *Courtesy of Bertrand Cocq* $350-450

This "lady" badger is still wearing her apron. *Courtesy of Bertrand Cocq* $275-400

A jockey appears on one side while a carriage driver appears on the other symbolizing sport and work. *Courtesy of Bertrand Cocq* $395-495

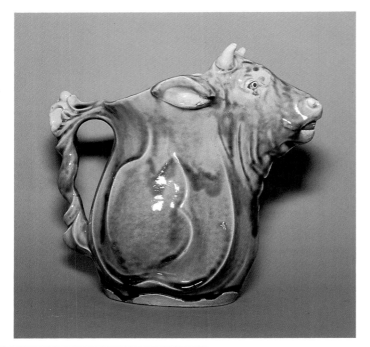

Bull figures appeared as paperweights and shelf ornaments, but not often as jugs. The handle on this jug is a sword wrapped in a cape. Lions appeared in ceramics occasionally in England, but not very often in France. This French jug of a lion has a lizard. *Courtesy of Bertrand Cocq* $400-500 each.

Boar's heads as tureens perhaps served as inspiration for this paté dish. *Britannia, Grays Antique Market, London* $2,200-2,600

The "comique troupier" entertained the troops in World War I. Modeled after Mr. Poulin who achieved fame during the war, the figure holds out his hand for donations. Other famous comedians included Dranem, Fragson, Mayol, and Ouvrard. *Courtesy of Bertrand Cocq* $500-600

This rooster-man is unique. The colors resemble those of Orchies, but the piece is unmarked. *Courtesy of Bertrand Cocq* $500-600

Very Provençal, this French woman carries her basket. *Photography by Jill Graham* $450-525

A tobacco jar of a "comique troupier." *Courtesy of M & G Bottero Antiquites, Nice* $150-195

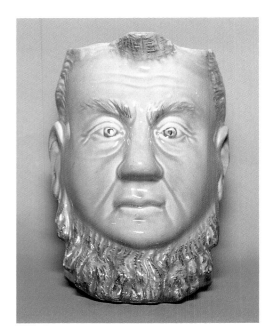

Some experts believe that this jug represents Jules Ferry who founded a school for children in France. Others believe it is President McKinley, noteworthy because of the McKinley Tariff Act of 1891. 8.5" high. Marked only with "depose" and an impressed number. *Courtesy of M & G Bottero Antiquites, Nice* $300-400

The origin of this jug is unknown, but the figure is Armand Fallieres, 1841-1931, who became the president of the French Republic in 1906. *Courtesy of Jacques Salzard* $400-550

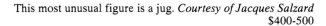

This most unusual figure is a jug. *Courtesy of Jacques Salzard* $400-500

An unusual monk figure who appears to be hiding something (a bottle?) under his robe. *Courtesy of M & G Bottero Antiquites, Nice* $300-400

Much of the continental majolica is unmarked or marked only with three- or four-digit numbers. In all probability these pieces are Austro-Hungarian. These unmarked pieces include figures on candlesticks, vases, tobacco jars, strikers, and wall pockets. Because majolica dealers and collectors generally refer to these pieces by the name of the figure, they are included in this study even though the figure accounts for only about 50% of the piece.

At the International Exhibition of 1862 in London, a reviewer of Austro-Hungarian pottery noted that of the fifty-four manufacturers attending, one half were from the Austro-Hungarian area and ten of them were situated around Carlsbad. He continued by stating:

> The production of common pottery occupies 8500 potters in all parts of the empire. In some places . . . a multitude of potteries will be found crowded together, but no extensive establishments have till now carried this branch of the industry.[1]

The lack of marks or the inconsistency of numerical markings resulted from a conglomerate of cottage industries. Designs may have been manufactured by several industries at the same time. Many of these pieces served as premiums or prizes at the fairs which were becoming increasingly popular. Their charm is unquestionable, however. Though not finely potted and often painted indiscriminately, they reveal an unmistakable creativity which attracts collectors today. As whimsical as their English and French counterparts, they offer the collector a variety from which to choose.

Cottage industries on the continent accounted for the manufacture of the largest majority of smoking paraphernalia. According to nineteenth-century customs, the men would retire after dinner to an appointed room where they could smoke in comfort without fear of offending the ladies. All sorts of smoking items appeared on the market, often in majolica. Smoking sets, ashtrays, strikers, and tobacco jars appeared both in England and on the continent. The majority of the tobacco jars average 5" to 7" high. Many of the figures on tobacco jars are either drinking, smoking, or playing an instrument.

Other continental items include vases, candlesticks, and figurines. Many of these had figures of shepherd boys and girls in keeping with contemporary designs. Other popular patterns included children playing.

This stork with a book is a tobacco jar. *Courtesy of Everett Grist* $295-350

This well-dressed duck and these proud dogs are all tobacco jars. *Courtesy of Everett Grist* $250-350

This cow with an umbrella and the frogs are familiar examples of tobacco jars. *Courtesy of Everett Grist* $275-350 cow; $385-475 smoking frog; $395-495 croaking frog.

A rather unusual fish in a jacket tobacco jar. 8.5" high. *Courtesy of Majolica Auctions by Michael G. Strawser* $500-600

The figure of the hippo appeared in ancient Egyptian tomb furnishings dating back to 1900 B.C. 5.25" high. Here the hippo is a tobacco jar. *Courtesy of Everett Grist* $385-495

The elephant tobacco jar is dressed somewhat like the bulldog tobacco jar. *Courtesy of Everett Grist* $385-495

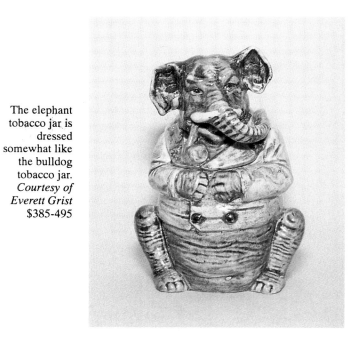

The delicate features of the resting boy add to the charm of this tobacco jar. *Courtesy of Everett Grist* $175-300

Women appeared occasionally as tobacco jars. *Courtesy of Everett Grist* $125-185

Stereotypes that the nineteenth century consumer would probably recognize. *Courtesy of M & G Bottero Antiquites, Nice* $150-275

The man's collar on this tobacco jar has "Boer" on it, obviously intended for a particular market. 6.75" high. *Courtesy of M & G Bottero Antiquites, Nice* $200-300

The hats of these faces are lids for the tobacco jars. *Courtesy of Everett Grist* $185-275

This fellow appears up to mischief! *Courtesy of Everett Grist* $175-250

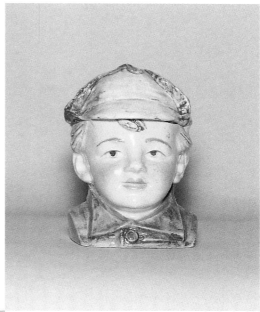

The bearded man, the jockey, and the motorist were typical figures of the nineteenth century. *Courtesy of Everett Grist* $185-275

The popular figure of the monk even appeared as a tobacco jar. *Courtesy of Everett Grist* $150-195

The big-eared "tough guys" appeared on several versions of tobacco jars. *Courtesy of Everett Grist* $185-295

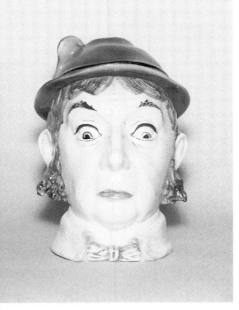

These faces express surprise. *Courtesy of Everett Grist* $250-350

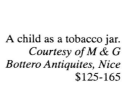

A child as a tobacco jar. *Courtesy of M & G Bottero Antiquites, Nice* $125-165

Jesters and clowns became popular because of the circus around the turn of the twentieth century. Naturally they appeared in ceramics. *Courtesy of Everett Grist* $150-225 jester; $200-350 clown.

Black faces with matte finish and gloss finish appeared as tobacco jars. *Courtesy of Everett Grist* $425-595 with hat; $250-400 other

These pieces marked "Belgium" were part of a tobacco set. Lids on these are often missing, especially on the smaller one. *Courtesy of Bertrand Cocq* $55-200 depending on size and lid.

The *Des Indes* designs included Middle Eastern figures as well as Indians. *Courtesy of Everett Grist* $185-295
86.410

Collectors refer to strikers according to the figure upon them. *Courtesy of Majolica Auctions by Michael G. Strawser* $150-250

The figure of the banjo player appeared on strikers 5" high and as life-size figurines. *Courtesy of Bertrand Cocq* $395-495

A candleholder, match holder, and striker all in one! *Courtesy of Ben Gary* $350-425

Indians also appeared on match holders. *Courtesy of Majolica Auctions by Michael G. Strawser* $250-395

Figurines, Vases, and Miscellaneous

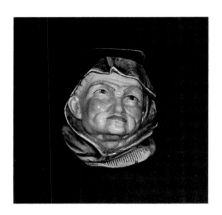

A monk figure as a bottle and another as a wall mount. *Courtesy of Majolica Auctions by Michael G. Strawser* $200-300

The charm of well-dressed figures must have appealed to the nineteenth century middle class. *Courtesy of Majolica Auctions by Michael G. Strawser* $825-1,100 busts 14" high; $275-350 figurines 14" high; $125-195 candleholder.

Common designs included the lady with the fan and a cat. Here they are presented together. *Courtesy of Majolica Auctions by Michael G. Strawser* $75-100

This lady is very fashionable. *Courtesy of Leprechaun Antiques* $95-125

Love of children and animals indicated a Victorian lady of class: perhaps one reason for the popularity of majolica figures like these. *Courtesy of Majolica Auctions by Michael G. Strawser* $95-150

A most unusual pastry brush holder. 5" high. *Courtesy of Brandon S. Queen* $200-325

This shepherdess vase had a companion piece (not shown here) with a shepherd boy on it. $100-140

"Waist Up" figures appeared on all sizes of ceramics, from strikers to this unique life-size banjo player with real strings on the instrument. *Courtesy of Anne Ford Associates, Inc.* $13,000-15,000

This gnome looks like he just came from work. *Courtesy of Majolica Auctions by Michael G. Strawser* $110-150

Chapter Nine

Beware of Reproductions!

The popularity of a number of majolica figures continues today. Many contemporary majolica manufacturers openly reproduce some of the most popular animal and human figurals from the nineteenth and early twentieth centuries. It is a testament to the creativity of the original designers that today's manufacturers reproduce these designs. Most manufacturers clearly mark their reproductions with no intent to defraud or deceive. However, unscrupulous individuals take advantage of any situation, so it is incumbent upon the collector and dealer to know if the piece being offered is original. Learning the characteristics of the originals, as well as the reproductions, may save one from a costly mistake.

The distinction between copy and reproduction is important to make at this point. A copy is an imitation of the original made during the same period. With repeated use molds lost their distinctive edging and detail, making them less desirable for the major manufacturers who then sold them to smaller firms. In addition, workers migrated from one factory to another, often taking their molds, designs, or simply their ideas with them. Since this migration was part of the overall atmosphere of the nineteenth century, copies are often as valuable as originals. Some collectors enjoy seeing the variety of a design. Because decorators painted each piece by hand, all pieces have distinctive features. The pieces made by an English factory, even though they are from the same mold, have a very different appearance than those from a French factory, for example.

Reproductions, on the other hand, are manufactured years later. Although reproductions may make a figure affordable, they will not increase in value, unlike the original or the copy. Generally inexpensive, reproductions can be used and enjoyed, though in a very different way from the original.

Only by knowing the telltale qualities of the original factories can a collector or dealer protect himself from fraud. Most reproductions lack the subtlety displayed by the nineteenth century designers and decorators. Moreover, they lack detail. A knowledge of coloring, weight, and particulars of the original will go far in protecting individuals from deceit. Spend time handling originals and notice their features. Talk to reputable dealers and collectors who are generally willing to spend time with interested individuals.

Consider the differences in the English productions as compared to the French or the continental. Examine the crazing which occurs with age. Since the porous clay body of a majolica piece dries faster than the glazed exterior, it causes slight cracks in the glaze. Crazing is natural, especially on majolica. Without it, the piece may have little or no age. The exception, of course, is parian or earthenware with a majolica glaze. Parian and some earthenware consists of a less porous clay than majolica. Consequently, it dries and ages much the same as the glaze, so the crazing will be very slight.

Sometimes crazing is added to reproductions. In this case the lines or cracks will appear very evenly distributed. The crazing lines are colored or painted as a part of the overall design. Do not be fooled into thinking this piece is old. Painted crazing was popular on the 1920s' reproductions of some of the old Staffordshire toby jugs. Today manufacturers use it on some reproductions of majolica figures. With some practice one learns to detect reproduction crazing.

One of the popular Sarreguemines character jugs currently being reproduced and sold in England is the "two-faced" jug. Since the reproduction is unmarked, it would be easy to mistake for the original unless one knew that Sarreguemines marked all of its products. Also, on the reproduction the phrase is in English rather than French. In addition, by examining the painted crazing, a knowledgeable buyer would become suspicious.

The Faïencerie d'Art de la Sorgue in France is currently reproducing at least fourteen of the most popular French figurals from a variety of French nineteenth-century firms. The Faïencerie marks its products which have even become somewhat collectible in their own right. However, some dealers in the United States are deceiving customers with these pieces, either intentionally or unintentionally. Because there has been a very real shortage of information on the French factories, buyers do not recognize the originals. Though the initials of the company manufacturing the reproductions, F.F.A.S., are clearly marked in all caps and "Made in France" also appears on the underside of the base, unscrupulous dealers have "weathered" these pieces and sell them as originals.

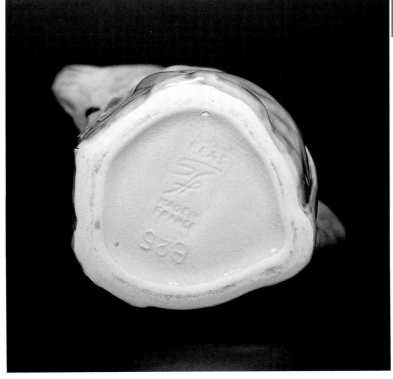

159

By becoming familiar with the distinctive features of the original manufacturers, the collector and the dealer will find it easier to identify the originals and prevent being deceived. The F.F.A.S. reproductions have a limited palette which includes pale mustard, soft crimson, light yellow, muted gray, golden brown, and a characteristic aqua. All pieces have one or more of these colors. In addition, the reproductions are slightly smaller than the originals. These jugs have the letter "B" followed by a one- or two-digit number on the base. Reproductions include the St. Clément duck (which was made in several sizes), elephant, parrot (not the cockatoo), and rooster; the Onnaing pig waiter, duck, rooster ("le Gaulois"), monkey, and railroader; the Sarreguemines dog on its haunches; the Orchies badger with an umbrella and pig with a ham; the Fives-Lille pipe-smoking frog; and the unattributed lion with a lizard in its mouth.

Other firms are manufacturing reproductions. St. Clément is reproducing figurals from its own molds and from old Sarreguemines molds. These new pieces are very easy to identify because they are light weight with sharp colors and little detail. Moreover, they are clearly marked. St. Clément also reproduced the Tessier man on the barrel in the 1950s, but it too was clearly marked and lacked in detail.

marked, inexperienced dealers or those not familiar with toby jugs incorrectly identify them as majolica. These jugs have an orange tint to the skin tone: a tint never seen on majolica.

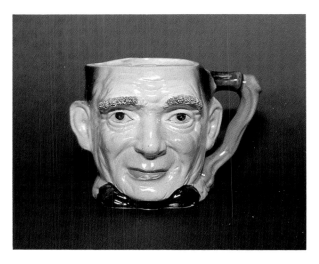

On occasion the author has seem these Japanese jugs tagged as majolica with a price to match. If a piece has "bushy" facial hair, it is not majolica.

This 1950s St. Clément reproduction of the Tessier man on the barrel lacks any definition. *Courtesy of M & G Bottero Antiquites, Nice*

The Coventry Company in the United States began reproducing a few of the Sarreguemines-type character jugs in the 1950s and presumably continued until the firm closed in the late 1960s.

On several occasions the author has seen some Japanese tobies made around the 1940s sold as majolica toby jugs. The Japanese tobies originally had paper labels which have disappeared over the years. Because they are un-

The now defunct Coventry Corporation in the United States copied several Sarreguemines-type designs and gave each a name, marked on the base.

Each jug was clearly marked and even had a name printed on the bottom. Other reproductions of French jugs include the Onnaing pig waiter made by a Portuguese firm. The pig has painted features. While quite charming, it is nonetheless a reproduction.

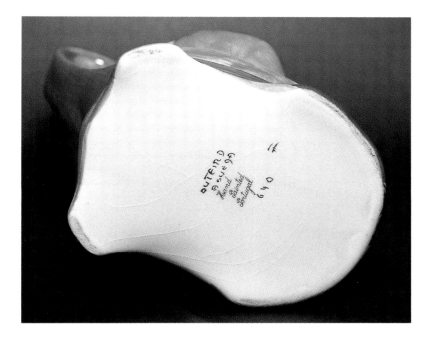

This copy of the Onnaing pig waiter came from Portugal.

Reproductions have a valid place in the market. However, it is up to the buyer to know the difference between a reproduction and an original.

This English reproduction of the Sarreguemines two-faced jug has an English rather than French phrase around the bottom and painted crazing. The phrase reads: "When I'm full I'm happy - When I'm Empty I'm Sad." *Courtesy of "Marty"*

In conclusion, this book is intended to aid collectors and dealers in developing an appreciation of the creativity and charm offered by majolica figures. They add interest to any decor, from country to traditional to contemporary. I also hope to give readers an ability to judge the authentic majolica figures from the reproductions in the marketplace. For more than twenty years I have collected and enjoyed figurals, but because of the dearth of information, I have made many errors. After learning from mistakes and from my years of research, I would like to give others the benefit of my efforts. Hopefully I can help prevent readers from making many of the same mistakes I have made.

In addition, I hope to impart a real love of these figures and an appreciation for the factories that made them. It pains me to see figures misrepresented because factory records have been destroyed over the years. The designers and firms who toiled to create humorous, witty, or contemporary statements deserve to be recognized for their labors. I hope that I have offered information that readers will find useful and perhaps will inspire them to continue my research, for I have only scratched the surface.

Within the field of majolica figures much variety exists, not only in cost and availability, but in quality and subject matter. The beginning collector, as well as the advanced, will have a chance to acquire delightful pieces. There truly exists something for everyone!

Decorating with majolica figures gives a warmth and charm to any room.

Majolica figures catch the eye when grouped together!

Endnotes

Introduction

1. Endnote citations are placed at the end of the discussions in all chapters. Carl W. Drepperd, *Victorian: The Cinderella of Antiques* (Garden City, NJ: Doubleday & Co., Inc., 1950), 5.
2. Nicholas M. Dawes, *Majolica* (New York: Crown Publishers, Inc., 1990), 18-20.
3. Daniel Pool, *What Jane Austen Ate and Charles Dickens Knew: From Fox Hunting to Whist—The Facts of Daily Life in Nineteenth-Century England* (New York, Simon & Schuster, 1993), 37.
4. Eugen Weber, *France: Fin De Siècle* (Cambridge, MA: The Belnap Press of Harvard University, 1986), 165.
5. Dreppard, *Cinderella,* 146.
6. Aldon B. Bell, *London in the Age of Dickens* (Norman, OK: University of Oklahoma Press, 1967), 141.
7. Pool, *What Jane Austen Ate*, 61.
8. Stuart E. Prall and David Harris Willson, *A History of England: 1603 to the Present*, 4th ed., Vol. 2 (Ft. Worth: Holt, Rinehart & Winston, Inc., 1991), 676-677.
9. Weber, *Fin De Siècle*, 159, 197, 203.

Chapter One

1. Diana Imber, *Collecting European Delft and Faïence* (New York: Frederick A. Praeger Publishing, 1968), 17.
2. Dreppard, *Cinderella*, 8.
3. Hugh Wakefield, *Victorian Pottery* (New York: Thomas Nelson & Sons, 1962), 47-48, 51-52.
4. Harold Osborne, ed., *The Oxford Companion to Art* (Oxford: The Clarendon Press, 1970), 945.
5. Imber, *Collecting*, 17-19.
6. L. G. G. Ramsey, ed., *The Connoisseur New Guide to Antique English Pottery, Porcelain and Glass* (New York: E. P. Dutton & Co., Inc., 1961), 80.

Chapter Two

1. Osborne, *Oxford Companion to Art*, 1025, 11.
2. Ferdinando Reyna, *A Concise History of Ballet* (New York: Grosset & Dunlap, 1964), 98, 122.

3. Joseph Machlis, *The Enjoyment of Music: An Introduction to Perceptive Listening* (New York: W.W. Norton & Co., 1977), 86-88, 98-114, 179.
4. "Mr. Dickens' Desk," *House Beautiful*, March 1992, 66.
5. Weber, *Fin De Siècle*, 144-147.
6. Sophie and Robert Lehr, "Continental Potteries," in Marilyn G. Karmason with Joan B. Stacke, *Majolica: A Complete History and Illustrated Survey* (New York: Harry N. Abrams, Inc., 1989), 186.
7. William Hardy, *A Guide to Art Nouveau Style* (Secaucus, NJ: Chartwell Books, Inc., 1986, rpt. 1988), 11-26.

Chapter Three

1. Paul Atterbury, ed., *The Parian Phenomenon: A Survey of Victorian Parian Porcelain Statuary & Busts* (Somerset, England: Richard Dennis, 1989), 48-55.
2. Karmason with Stacke, *Majolica*, 33.
3. Karmason with Stacke, 11.
4. Leslie Bockol, *Victorian Majolica* (Atglen, PA: Schiffer Publishing Ltd., 1996), 53.
5. Joan Jones, *Minton: The First Two Hundred Years of Design & Production* (Shrewsbury, England: Swan Hill Press, 1993), 140; Karmason with Stacke, *Majolica*, 52.
6. Jeffrey B. Snyder and Leslie Bockol, *Majolica: American & European Wares* (Atglen, PA: Schiffer Publishing Ltd., 1994), 109; Dawes, *Majolica*, 88.
7. Jones, *Minton*, 154.
8. Dawes, *Majolica,* 87-91.
9. John P. Cushion, *Animals in Pottery and Porcelain* (New York: Crown Publishers, Inc., 1974), 31-45.
10. Victoria Bergesen, *Majolica: British, Continental, and American Wares*, 1851-1915 (London: Barrie & Jenkins, 1989), 74-76; Karmason with Stacke, *Majolica*, 88-89.
11. Bergesen, 72.
12. Karmason with Stacke, *Majolica*, 105.

Chapter Four

1. Bergesen, *Majolica*, 70.
2. Snyder and Bockol, *Majolica*, 97.

3. William O. Steele, "The Curious Case of Cherokee Clay," *Historical Review and Antique Digest* (Winter, 1974), 11-13.
4. Bergesen, *Majolica*, 61.
5. Karmason with Stacke, *Majolica*, 128.
6. Bergesen, *Majolica*, 141.
7. Geoffrey A. Godden, *Encyclopedia of British Pottery and Porcelain Marks* (New York: Bonanza Books, 1964), 72.
8. Karmason with Stacke, 121.

Chapter Five

1. *Regard Historique et Technique: Les Collections du Musée de Sarreguemines*, Service éducatif du musée de Sarreguemines (November, 1993), 9-10.
2. Pierre Faveton, *Les Barbotines* (Paris: Massin Editeur, 1990), 49-50.
3. *Regard,* 10-11.
4. Faveton, *Barbotines*, 51-52.
5. "À la redécouverte de la faïencerie de Sarreguemines," *Circuit Touristique*, 7.
6. Bergesen, *Majolica*, 112.
7. *Regard*, 13.
8. Information not otherwise noted, in large part from personal interviews with Mr. Emile Decker, consevateur, and Mr. Christian Thevenin, assistant conservateur of the Musée De Sarreguemines as well as discussions with Mr. Denis Bour, president of Les Amis Du Musée Et Des Arts De Sarreguemines in Sarreguemines, France.
9. Alan D. Eames, *Secret Life of Beer: Legends, Lore & Little Known Facts* (Pownal, VT: Storey Communications, Inc., 1995), 15-20.
10. Charles Dickens, *Barnaby Rudge* (New York: Dodd, Mead & Company, 1944), 20.
11. Christopher Hibbert, *The Horizon Book of Daily Life in Victorian England* (New York: American Heritage Publishing Co., Inc., 1975), 70.
12. Pool, *What Jane Austen Ate*, 210.
13. Eames, *Secret Life*, 61.
14. Vic Schuler, *Collecting British Toby Jugs,* 2nd. ed. (London: Francis Joseph Publications, 1994), 8-10.
15. *Chefs-D'Oeuvres de la Faïence du Musée de Saint-Omer* (Musée de l'Hôtel Sandelin, 1988), 75.
16. Schuler, *Toby Jugs*, 60.
17. Robert E. Röntgen, *Marks on German, Bohemian and Austrian Porcelain: 1710 to the Present* (Atglen, PA: Schiffer Publishing Ltd., 1981), 490.
18. Karmason with Stacke, *Majolica*, 180-182; Faveton, *Barbotines*, 56-58.
19. *Faïencerie D'Onnaing (Nord): Ancienne Société Mouzin Frères Et Cie.* Company catalog. No date.
20. Letter from a member of the Assemblée Nationale, Republique Française in Paris to Mr. Bertrand Cocq, December 21, 1986.
21. *Manufacture de Faïences & Porcelaines de St. Amand, Homage & Orchies, Fondee en 1818.* Company catalog. No date.
22. Karmason with Stacke, *Majolica*, 189; Robert Lehr, personal interview, April, 1995.

Chapter Six

1. Faveton, *Barbotines*, 78.
2. Gilles Blieck, *Faïencerie Artistique de Fives-Lille: Photographie sur Porcelaine, Faïence, Gres, Poterie.* Travaux du Groupe de Recherches et d'Etudes sur la Céramique dans le Nord-Pas-De-Calais (Nord-Ouest Archéologie, 1993), 21-46.
3. Karmason with Stacke, *Majolica*, 188-189; Faveton, *Barbotines*, 69.
4. Millicent S. Mali, *French Faïence* (United Printing, 1986), 71-72.

Chapter Seven

1. Röntgen, *Marks*, 415, 385.

Chapter Eight

1. Joe Horowitz, M.D., *Figural Tobacco Jars: An Introduction and Illustrated Guide to Values* (Baltimore: FTJ Publications, 1994), 2.

Bibliography

Pottery Resources

Atterbury, Paul J., ed. *European Pottery and Porcelain.* New York: Mayflower Books, USA, 1979.

Atterbury, Paul J., ed. *The Parian Phenomenon: A Survey of Victorian Parian Porcelain Statuary & Busts.* Somerset, England: Richard Dennis, 1989.

Battie, David and Michael Turner.*The Guide to 19th and 20th Century Pottery.* Woodbridge, Suffolk, England: Antique Collectors' Club Ltd., 1987; rpt. 1990.

Blacker, J. F. *The A.B.C. of Collecting Old English Pottery.* London: Stanley Paul and Co. No date.

Blieck, Gilles. *Faïencerie Artistique de Fives-Lille: Photographie sur Porcelaine, Faïence, Gres, Poterie.* Travaux du Groupe de Recherches et d'Études sur la Céramique dans le Nord-Pas-De-Calais. Béthune, France: Nord-ouest Archéologie, 1993.

Bockol, Leslie. *Victorian Majolica.* Atglen, PA: Schiffer Publishing Ltd., 1996.

Chaffers, William. *Collector's Handbook of Marks and Monograms on Pottery and Porcelain.* Los Angeles: Borden Publishing Company. No date.

Charleston, Robert J., ed. *World Ceramics.* New York: The Hamlyn Publishing Group Ltd., 1968.

Chefs-D'oeuvres De La Faïence Du Musee De Saint-Omer, Musée de l'Hôtel Sandelin, 1988.

Cox, Warren E. *The Book of Pottery and Porcelain.* Vol. I and II. New York: Crown Publishers, Inc., 1944.

Cushion, John P. *Animals in Pottery and Porcelain.* New York: Crown Publishers, Inc., 1974.

— and William B. Honey. *Handbook of Pottery & Porcelain Marks.* 4th ed. London: Faber & Faber, 1980.

Dawes, Nicholas M. *Majolica.* New York: Crown Publishers, Inc., 1990.

Decker, Emile and Christian Thevenin. *La Majolique de Sarreguemines.* Sarreguemines: Association des Amis du Musée de Sarreguemines, 1990.

Faïencerie d'Onnaing (Nord): Ancienne Société Mouzin Frère et Cie. Company catalog. No date.

Faveton, Pierre. *Les Barbotines.* Paris: Massin Editeur, 1990.

Faÿ-Hallé, Antoinette. *La Faïence en Europe.* Paris: Flammarion, 1988.

Field, Rachael. *MacDonald Guide to Buying Antique Pottery and Porcelain.* Radnor, PA: Wallace-Homestead Book Company, 1987.

Finer, Ann and George Savage. *The Selected Letters of Josiah Wedgwood.* London: Cory, Adams and MacKay, Ltd., 1965.

Gilchrist, Brenda, gen. ed. *The Smithsonian Illustrated Library of Antiques: Pottery.* New York: Cooper-Hewitt Museum, 1981.

Godden, Geoffrey A. *The Concise Guide to British Pottery and Porcelain.* London: Barrie and Jenkins, 1973.

—. *Encyclopedia of British Pottery and Porcelain Marks.* New York: Bonanza Books, 1964.

Goreley, Jean. *The Collector's Library: Wedgwood.* New York: Gramercy Publishing Co., 1950.

Halfpenny, Pat. *English Earthenware Figures: 1740-1840.* Woodbridge, Suffolk, England: Antique Collectors' Club, 1991; 2nd ed. 1995.

Hall, John. *Staffordshire Pottery Figures.* New York: The World Publishing Company, 1972.

Hartman, Urban. *Porcelain and Pottery Marks.* New York: privately published, 1943.

Haslom, Malcolm. *Connoisseur's Library: Pottery.* London: Orbis Publishing, 1972.

Hoover, Mary W. "Reminiscences in Collecting Majolica." *Hobbies:The Magazine for Collectors.* (March, 1939): 69-70.

Horowitz, Joe, M.D. *Figural Tobacco Jars: An Introduction and Illustrated Guide to Values.* Baltimore: FTJ Publishing, 1994.

Imber, Diana. *Collecting European Delft and Faïence.* New York: Frederick A. Praeger, Publishing, 1968.

Jewitt, Llewellynn. *The Ceramic Art of Great Britain.* London: J. S. Virtue and Company, 1878; rev. 1883.

Jones, Joan. *Minton: The First Two Hundred Years of Design and Production.* Shrewsbury, England: Swan Hill Press, 1993.

Karmason, Marilyn G. with Joan B. Stacke. *Majolica: A Complete History and Illustrated Survey.* New York: Harry N. Abrams, Inc., 1989.

Katz-Marks, Mariann. *Majolica Pottery: An Identification and Value Guide.* Paducah, KY: Collector Books, 1986.

—. *Majolica Pottery: An Identification and Value Guide.* Second Series. Paducah, KY: Collector Books, 1989.

—. *The Collector's Encyclopedia of Majolica: An Identification and Value Guide.* Paducah, KY: Collector Books, 1992.

Kovel, Ralph M. and Terry H. *Dictionary of Marks on Pottery and Porcelain.* New York: Crown Publishing, Inc., 1953.

—. *New Dictionary of Marks: Pottery and Porcelain 1850 to the Present.* New York: Crown Publishing, Inc., 1986.

Lee, Albert. *Portraits in Pottery.* Boston: The Stratford Company, 1931.

Lehner, Lois. *Lehner's Encyclopedia of U. S. Marks on Pottery, Porcelain and Clay.* Paducah, KY: Collector Books, 1988.

Lehr, Robert. "Barbotines des Massier à Vallauris." *Antiquitiés, beaux-arts, curiosités* (April-May 1987): 47-52.

Les Marques de Fabrique: Les Faïences de Sarreguemines. Sarreguemines, France: Association des Amis du Musée de Sarreguemines, 1990.

Lewis, Griselda. *Collector's History of English Pottery.* New York: Viking Press, 1969.

Little Romances of China. Syracuse, NY: privately printed for Onondaga Pottery Company, 1919.

Macht, Carol. *Classical Wedgwood Designs.* New York: Gramercy Publishing Company, 1957.

Manufacture de Faïences et Porcelaines: St. Amand, Hamage et Orchies. Company catalog. No date.

Moore, N. Hudson. *The Old China Book including Staffordshire, Wedgwood, Lustre and Other English Pottery and Porcelain.* New York: Tudor Publishing Company, 1903.

Paton, James. *Jugs: A Collector's Guide.* London: Souvenir Press Ltd., 1976.

Petersen, E. Paul and A. *Collector's Handbook to Marks on Porcelain and Pottery.* Green Farms, CT: Modern Books and Crafts, Inc., 1974.

Poole, Julia. *Plagiarism Personified?* Cambridge: Fitzwilliam Museum, 1986.

Ray, Marcia. *Collectible Ceramics: An Encyclopedia of Pottery and Porcelain for the American Collector.* New York: Crown Publishing, Inc., 1974.

Ramsey, L. G., ed. *The Connoisseur New Guide to Antique English Pottery, Porcelain and Glass.* New York: E. P. Dutton, Inc., 1961.

Regard Historique et Technique: Les Collections du Musée de Sarreguemines. Sarreguemines, France: Service éducatif du musée de Sarreguemines, 1993.

Rhodes, Daniel. *Clay and Glazes for the Potter.* New York: Chilton Book Company, 1957, rpt. 1968.

Rickerson, Wildey C. *Majolica: Collect It for Fun and Profit.* Chester, CT: The Pequot Press, 1972.

Röntgen, Robert E. *Marks on German, Bohemian and Austrian Porcelain: 1710 to the Present.* Atglen, PA: Schiffer Publishing Ltd., 1981.

Savage, George. *Ceramics for the Collector: An Introduction to Pottery and Porcelain.* London: Salisbury Square, 1949.

Scavizzi, Guiseppe. *Maiolica, Delft and Faïence.* Trans. Peter Locke. New York: The Hamlyn Publishing Group Limited, 1970.

Schneider, Mike. *Majolica.* Atglen, PA: Schiffer Publishing Ltd., 1990.

Schuler, Vic. *Collecting British Toby Jugs.* 2nd ed., London: Francis Joseph Publications, 1994.

Snyder, Jeffrey B. and Leslie Bockol. *Majolica: American and European Wares.* Atglen, PA: Schiffer Publishing Ltd., 1994.

Steele, William O. "The Curious Case of Cherokee Clay." *Historical Review and Antique Digest* (Winter 1974):11-13.

Thorn, C. Jordan. *Handbook of Old Pottery and Porcelain Marks.* New York: Tudor Publishing Company, 1947.

Wakefield, Hugh. *Victorian Pottery.* New York: Thomas Nelson and Sons, 1962.

Williams, Peter. *Wedgwood: A Collector's Guide.* Radnor, PA: Wallace-Homestead Book Company, 1992.

General Resources

Bell, Aldon B. *London in the Age of Dickens.* Norman, OK: University of Oklahoma Press, 1967.

Bond, Harold Lewis. *An Encyclopedia of Antiques.* New York: Tudor Publishing Company, 1945.

Brossard, Yvonne and Alain Jacob. *Sarreguemines.* Paris: Grou-Radenez, 1975.

Bumpus, Judith. *Impressionist Gardens.* New York: Barnes and Noble, 1990.

Chefs-D'Oeuvres de l'Art Grands Peintres: Renoir. Paris: Hachette. No date.

Carpenter, Rhys. *The Esthetic Basis of Greek Art.* Bloomington, IN: Indiana University Press, 1959.

Christensen, Erwin O. *The History of Western Art.* New York: The New American Library, 1959.

Costantino, Marcia. *Paul Gauguin.* New York: Barnes and Noble, 1994.

Crow, Duncan. *The Victorian Woman.* New York: Stein and Day, 1972.

Davenport, Millia. *The Book of Costume*, Vol. 1. New York: Crown Publishers, Inc., 1948.

Denvir, Bernard. *The Thames and Hudson Encyclopedia of Impressionism.* London: Thames and Hudson Ltd., 1990.

Drepperd, Carl W. *Victorian: The Cinderella of Antiques.* Garden City, NY: Doubleday and Company, Inc., 1950.

Durozoi, Gerard. *Matisse.* New York, Portland House, 1989.

Eames, Alan D. *Secret Life of Beer: Legends, Lore and Little Known Facts.* Pownal, VT: Storey Communications, Inc., 1995.

Gaunt, William. *English Painting.* London: Thames and Hudson, 1964, rpt. 1988.

Gere, Charlotte and Michael Whiteway. *Nineteenth Century Design: From Pugin to Mackintosh.* New York: Harry N. Abrams, Inc., 1994.

Gowing, Sir Lawrence, gen. ed. *A History of Art.* New York: Barnes and Noble, 1983; rev. 1995.

Grimaldi, Pierre. *L'Histoire Tourmentee de Village de Vallauris.* Vallauris, France: Association Le Vieux Vallauris. No date.

Grosline, Douglas. *What People Wore: A Visual History of Dress from Ancient Times to Twentieth Century America.* New York: Bonanza Books, 1951.

Hardy, William. *A Guide to Art Nouveau Style.* London: Chartwell Books, 1986; rpt. 1988.

Hartt, Frederick. *History of Italian Renaissance Art.* New York: Harry N. Abrams, Inc., 1969.

Heinrich, Christoph. *Monet.* New York: Barnes and Noble, 1996.

Herbert, Robert L. *Impressionism: Art, Leisure, and Parisian Society.* New Haven, CT: Yale University Press, 1988.

Hibbert, Christopher. *The Horizon Book of Daily Life in Victorian England.* New York: American Heritage Publishing Company, Inc., 1975.

Jenkins, Dorothy H. *A Treasure in the Junk Pile.* New York: Crown Publishers, Inc., 1963.

Langbaum, Robert. *The Victorian Age.* Chicago: Academy Publishing, 1969.

Machlis, Joseph. *The Enjoyment of Music: An Introduction to Perceptive Listening.* 4th ed. New York: W. W. Norton and Company, 1977.

"Mr. Dickens' Desk." *House Beautiful* (March 1992): 66-67.

Perry, Marvin, et al. *Western Civilization: Ideas, Politics and Society.* 4th ed. vol. 2. Boston: Houghton, Mifflin Company, 1992.

Pool, Daniel. *What Jane Austen Ate and Charles Dickens Knew: From Fox Hunting to Whist—The Facts of Daily Life in Nineteenth-Century England.* New York: Simon and Schuster, 1993.

Prall, Stuart E. and David Harris Willson. *A History of England: 1603 to the Present.* 4th ed. vol. 2. Ft. Worth, TX: Holt, Rinehart and Winston, Inc., 1991.

Reyna, Ferdinando. *A Concise History of Ballet.* New York: Grosset and Dunlap, 1964.

Smith, Paul. *Interpreting Cezanne.* New York: Stewart, Tabori and Chang, 1996.

Shull, Thelma. *Victorian Antiques.* Rutland, VT: Charles E. Tuttle Company, 1963.

Tobias, J. J. *Urban Crime in Victorian England.* New York: Schocken Books, 1967.

Trevelyn, G. M. *English Social History: A Survey of Six Centuries—Chaucer to Queen Victoria.* London: Longman Group, Ltd., 1944.

Uhl, Jean-Marie and Raymond Kraemer. *Sarreguemines: hier et avant hier.* Sarreguemines, France: Editions Pierron, 1993.

Youngs, Grederic A., Jr., et al. *The English Heritage.* 2nd ed. Arlington Heights, IL: Forum Press, Inc. 1988.

Weber, Eugen. *France: Fin de Siècle.* Cambridge, MA: The Belnap Press of Harvard University Press, 1986.

Index